The Ultimate Guide to Your Microscope

Shar Levine &
Leslie Johnstone

STERLING

New York / London
www.sterlingpublishing.com/kids

For Dr. Elaine Humphrey, a brilliant microscopist and a wonderful friend, without whose assistance, training, and expertise this book and many others would not have been possible.
—SL

For Mark, Chris, Nick, and Megan, who make every day interesting.
—LJ

All photomicrographs were created by the authors with the assistance of Dr. Elaine Humphrey.
All photographs were created by Shar Levine and Leslie Johnstone, except those of the slide preparations, which were done by El'ad Tzadok, the photographs of the microscopes © Carolina Biological Supply Company, used by permission, pages 14 and 16, and the teeth images by Dr. M. Schwartzman, pages 63 and 64.

Book Design by Ely Kim

STERLING and the distinctive Sterling logo are registered trademarks of Sterling Publishing Co., Inc.

Library of Congress Cataloging-in-Publication Data
Levine, Shar, 1953-
    The ultimate guide to your microscope / Shar Levine & Leslie Johnstone.
        p. cm.
    Includes index.
    ISBN-13: 978-1-4027-4329-0
    ISBN-10: 1-4027-4329-7
    1. Microscope—Juvenile literature. 2. Microscopy—Juvenile literature.
    I. Johnstone, Leslie. II. Title.
QH278.L487 2007
570.28'2--dc22

                                        2006100967

10   9   8

Published by Sterling Publishing Co., Inc.
387 Park Avenue South, New York, NY 10016
© 2008 by Shar Levine and Leslie Johnstone
Distributed in Canada by Sterling Publishing
C/o Canadian Manda Group, 165 Dufferin Street
Toronto, Ontario, Canada M6K 3H6
Distributed in the United Kingdom by GMC Distribution Services,
Castle Place, 166 High Street, Lewes, East Sussex, England BN7 1XU
Distributed in Australia by Capricorn Link (Australia) Pty. Ltd.
P.O. Box 704, Windsor, NSW 2756, Australia

Printed in China
All rights reserved

Sterling ISBN-13: 978-1-4027-4329-0
        ISBN-10: 1-4027-4329-7

For information about custom editions, special sales, premium and corporate purchases, please contact Sterling Special Sales Department at 800-805-5489 or specialsales@sterlingpub.com.

Contents

Preface

On TV shows and in movies, "scientists" peer into microscopes and, after making a few adjustments, proudly announce that they have just made a major discovery or solved a crime. There is no guarantee that the techniques in this book will give you results quite so dramatic. What you will learn, however, are the basics of creating your own **slides** and using a microscope.

No matter how good your eyesight may be, you still cannot see some of the curious and amazing things around you. With something as simple as a magnifying glass, you can begin to discover tiny beasts in pond water, or hidden pictures on your weekly allowance. With more powerful optics, like those found in even the most inexpensive microscopes, you can view the inner workings of a healthy snack such as celery, the roots of an onion growing in the back of your fridge, or the pollen on a flower that makes you sneeze. The things you see might even teach you the merits of brushing your teeth after you eat.

If you have never looked through the eyepiece of a microscope, or even seen a microscope slide (a **sample** placed on a thin piece of glass), this book is for you. That is not to say that expert **microscopists** (people who use microscopes for a living) won't learn something new. This book has information and projects for everyone.

Unlike other science activity books, in which you can immediately perform any experiment, this book recommends that you read the opening chapters so that you can identify the parts of the microscope, practice **focusing**, and learn how to prepare samples for viewing. This way you will have the skills and procedures you need to enjoy using your microscope.

The Internet has made the purchase of materials, including **chemicals**, accessible to the average person. These materials are used by professionals to create slides, but they are often not recommended for home use. Instructions and experiments that you or your parents download from the Internet also may not be safe. Extreme caution should be used when ordering materials or following experiments found on the Internet. Even some older microscopy books have materials that are no longer considered safe for use by children. If you or your parent is unsure of these instructions, please check with a high school science teacher, university instructor, or any other expert in the field before attempting these activities or using these supplies.

Rather than providing a drawing of what you might see using your microscope, we have made **photomicrographs** (pictures taken through a microscope) of each slide. We followed the exact techniques described in the book. If your slide does not match the image in the book, don't worry. Make several slides and see whether another one more closely resembles our image.

This book is just the beginning of your adventures with a microscope, and you will probably want to examine many more things than are described here.

We have not killed any creature imaged in this book. If you look on your window ledge, you may find flies, moths, spiders, wasps, or other simple creatures that, due to their short life span, have died of natural causes. If an insect is already dead, then studying it under a microscope won't harm it. Think of it this way: It has donated its body to science. It is also possible to view some living organisms without harming them, and then return them to their natural habitat. The main thing to remember is: Do not be cruel to any living thing.

Scientists keep **journals** or records of their inquiries. We have provided a form (see "Keeping a Journal" on page 25) that you can reproduce and complete to document your **specimens**. You can also use a computer to create your own personalized form. The journal will remind you where you found the specimen, how you prepared it, what you saw, and what you learned. You can even use your research as the basis for a science fair project.

Have fun! You are about to discover a new world around you.

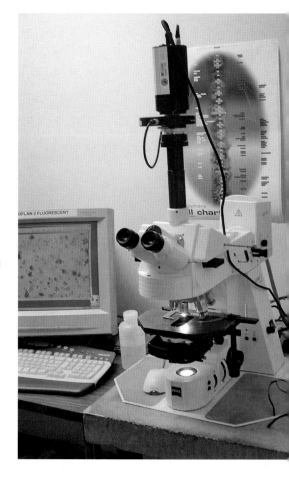

Authors' light microscope set up for making photomicrographs.

Part 1
Microscopes and Slides
Chapter 1
Before You Get Started

There is something mysterious, magical, and strange about the things you can see using a microscope. A single drop of water can contain living creatures. Pollen from a flower comes alive when sugar water is added to it. Even the money in your pocket has special features revealed only through the eyepiece of a microscope. Children of all ages will be fascinated studying everyday household and garden items.

Note to Parents and Teachers

We've tried to make the experiments as safe and foolproof as possible. Closely following the instructions will ensure the greatest chance of success. If sharp objects are needed, we strongly suggest that the child have an adult helper. Scientific words are defined the first time they are used; many also appear in the glossary at the back of the book.

The Ultimate Guide to Your Microscope is intended to teach children (and even adults) basic techniques and observation skills. We do not recommend growing any bacterial cultures or using human blood (not legal in many public schools) to make slides. These can be extremely dangerous if not handled correctly.

This book cannot answer every question a child might have about the specimens he or she views under the microscope. You can assist your child in learning more about what he or she has seen by searching the Internet, visiting a library, or even contacting a local university or college for more information.

If you do not own a microscope, try using a magnifying glass to perform some of the experiments. Also see the discussion in chapter 2, "I Don't Own a Microscope" (page 15). If you decide to buy, then universities, colleges, and even some businesses sell their used microscopes and offer them online through company or education Web sites. As with purchasing anything on the Internet, it's buyer beware, so order only from reputable vendors. You may want an expensive microscope with bells and whistles, but you don't need fancy equipment. When a child is learning, a simple microscope with good optics will be just fine.

Ocean bay at low tide.

With digital cameras now selling at reasonable prices, you may wish to attach one to your microscope to create permanent photos of your slides. You can add these photos to a journal that your child can keep to record his or her experiments.

If your child's school does not have a microscope and if you don't wish to purchase one, arrange a field trip to a local university or college, or ask an instructor from one of these institutions to speak at your child's school.

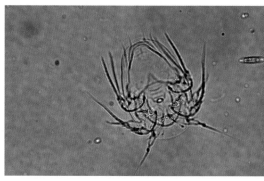

A nauplius seen in seawater with the light microscope at a magnification of x400.

Kids will be astonished to discover that their slides resemble those created by professionals. Be prepared for some major oohs and aahs and cooools as you and your child discover the microscopic world around you.

Safety First—Dos and Don'ts

Dos

1. Ask an adult before handling any materials, food, or equipment.
2. Have an adult perform any task involving sharp objects such as knives and razor blades. When you see the ☛ symbol, it means sharp tools or other sharp objects are used.
3. Read all the steps of the experiment carefully, gather your supplies, and be sure you know what to do before you begin the activity. If you are unsure of any step, ask an adult for assistance.
4. Always work in a well-ventilated area with good lighting.
5. Tie back long hair while you are working, and avoid wearing clothing with long, loose sleeves.
6. Keep your work area clean and wipe up spills immediately.
7. Wash your hands and work area after performing the experiments.
8. Tell an adult immediately if you hurt yourself in any way.
9. Keep all supplies, tools, chemicals, and experiments out of the reach of small children and animals.
10. Have an adult assist you with any Internet searches for information. Do not give out personal information, and do not try to perform any experiment found on the Internet without an adult's permission and direct supervision.

Don'ts

1. If you are allergic or sensitive to any foods or other substances such as mold or dust, do not use them to perform an experiment.
2. Do not taste, eat, or drink any of the materials associated with the experiments.
3. Do not kill or be cruel to any living creature in your experiments.
4. Never look at the sun or another strong source of light directly or through your magnifying lens or microscope.

List of Equipment

Before you get started, have the following basic supplies and equipment handy. Individual experiments require additional supplies that can be found, for the most part, in and around your home or at a grocery or other store. Before you begin an experiment or activity, gather all the materials that you need to do it. Make sure you have an adult helper, particularly when preparing to use any sharp objects or handle any equipment.

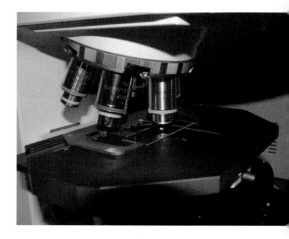

Revolving nosepiece of authors' light microscope with a slide on the stage.

Basics Supplies You Will Need

- microscope
- slides
- cover slips
- tweezers
- eyedropper
- lens paper
- notebook
- pen and pencil
- stage micrometer (or clear plastic ruler)
- microtome (see page 36 for instructions and supplies for making your own)
- razor knife (to be used by an adult)
- nail polish
- scissors

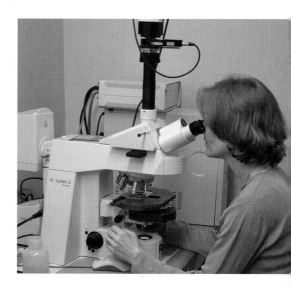

Author Leslie Johnstone at the microscope.

Microscopes and Slides

Chapter 2

Light, Lenses, and Microscopes

Microscopes use light to allow you to see tiny objects. The light from the lightbulb or mirror in your microscope travels through lenses that bend the light to magnify the image of your specimen while allowing you to focus the image of your sample so you can see it clearly. Let's look at how this works.

Light

Light is a form of energy that behaves like waves, much like the waves you see at the beach. If you drop a stone into still water, you will see waves moving outward in a series of circles from where you have dropped the stone. Light coming from a light source, like a lightbulb, also moves outward in waves from the source. Light waves travel very quickly, about 186,000 miles (300,000 kilometers [km]) per second, if they are going through the air. When light goes through other materials, such as the glass used to make lenses, it travels more slowly. Lenses make use of this change in the speed of light to cause the light to bend, or diffract. When the light is bent by the lenses, it can make objects appear larger, smaller, or even upside down.

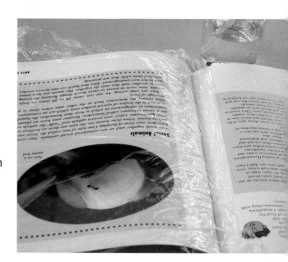

Try This

Place a piece of plastic wrap on top of a piece of a page in this book or a newspaper. Place a drop of water on the plastic wrap and try reading the words. How do the letters change?

Place a drop of water on the plastic wrap.

The drop of water acts as a lens.

Lenses

Lenses can be made of any clear material, such as glass or plastic, or even diamond. Lenses are available in several different shapes, but the ones in microscopes are usually a shape called *convex*. Convex lenses are thinner on the edges and thicker in the middle. These lenses can either make objects appear larger or make them turn upside down. Light microscopes usually contain 2 or more of these lenses, one near the sample, called the objective lens, and the other near your eye, called the ocular lens.

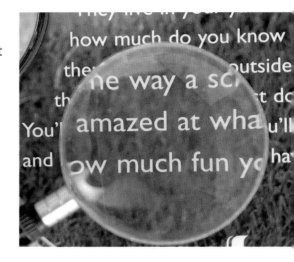

The effect of a convex lens—magnification.

Try This

Place this book on the floor, and then place a convex lens on top of this page. The easiest convex lens to use is a magnifying glass, or you can try this with different kinds of prescription eyeglasses. Hold the edges of the lens between your fingers, keeping your arm stretched out. Look at the words on the page, then slowly bring the lens away from the page and toward your eye. What happens to the image of the words you can see on the page? Bring the lens all the way up to your eye. Does anything else happen to the image of the words?

Here the lens turns the image upside down—inversion.

Identifying Your Microscope

What Kind of Microscope Do I Have?

Which microscope does yours most closely resemble?

The microscope on the top is a **light microscope**. The light in this case comes from below the sample. Because the light from a light microscope must shine through the sample in order for you to view it, the sample must be sliced very, very thin and must be very small. To best observe a slide, you may have to **stain** your sample. This means you may have to add **dye** or **ink** to your sample to outline the structures that are hard to see. Light microscopes are also known as **compound microscopes** because they have more than one lens. Simple microscopes have one lens—a magnifying lens is really a type of simple microscope. Compound microscopes have two lenses that are arranged so that light has to pass through both lenses before reaching your eye.

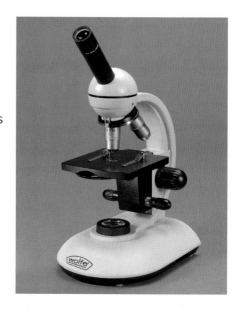

Light or compound microscope.
© Carolina Biological Supply Company, used by permission.

The microscope on the bottom is called a **dissecting microscope**. The word *dissecting* means to cut apart, but using this kind of microscope does not require you to cut anything. A dissecting microscope is used to examine things that are too thick or big to look at using a light microscope. The advantage of a dissecting microscope over a light microscope is that you don't have to slice a sample really thin in order to properly view it, and you don't have to stain your sample with dyes or inks. Basically, the microscope acts as a giant magnifying glass and allows you to see fine detail on the surface of your sample. Because the light usually comes from above the sample, you will see everything in bright colors. The disadvantage of using a dissecting microscope is that you cannot see what is inside things, and the dissecting microscope will generally not enlarge samples as much as a light microscope will. Light can also come from below the sample to aid the visualization in a dissecting microscope. The beauty of a

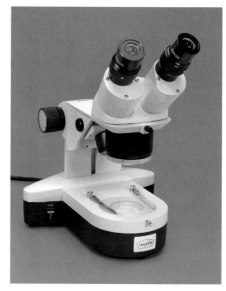

Dissecting microscope.
© Carolina Biological Supply Company, used by permission.

Easter lily pollen seen through a light microscope x200.

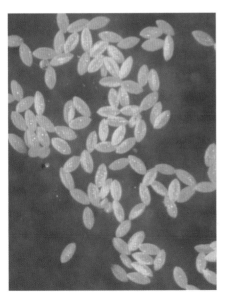

Lily pollen seen through a dissecting microscope.

dissecting microscope is that illumination can come from all around the specimen and not just through the specimen.

Compare the photomicrographs at left: The one above is a picture of pollen taken using a light microscope. The one below it is a picture of the same pollen taken using a dissecting microscope. The dissecting microscope's image shows the color, but you cannot see the detail of the pollen. Using a light microscope, you get greater detail, but it is hard to see the exact color of the pollen.

I Don't Own a Microscope

Which kind of microscope should I buy?

The first question you and your parents should answer is this: What kind of things do I want to study or examine? If you like to look at samples such as leaves, coins, or mineral specimens, and you like to see things in color, then you might want a dissecting microscope. If, however, you like working in fine detail with very tiny objects, and you don't mind creating tissue-thin samples, a light microscope would be the choice for you.

Microscope Basics

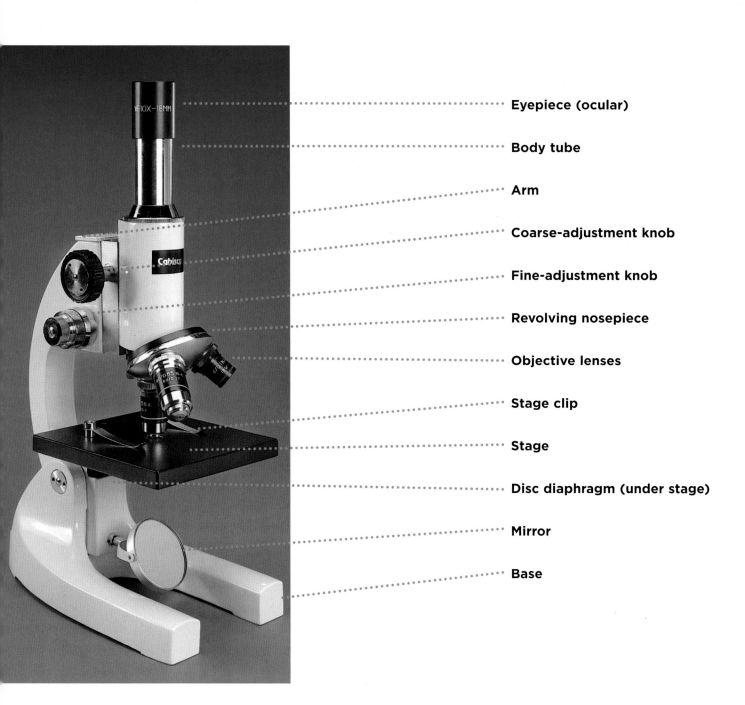

Eyepiece (ocular)

Body tube

Arm

Coarse-adjustment knob

Fine-adjustment knob

Revolving nosepiece

Objective lenses

Stage clip

Stage

Disc diaphragm (under stage)

Mirror

Base

Parts of a light microscope.
© Carolina Biological Supply Company,
used by permission.

Microscope Parts (Light Microscope)

A. The **eyepiece (ocular)** is the part of the microscope closest to your eye, through which you look. It contains the ocular lens, which makes the image produced by the objective lenses larger. Microscopes that have 2 eyepieces, each with an ocular lens, are called **binocular microscopes.** The ocular lenses can be labeled with different magnifications, for example, 5x or 10x (meaning the eyepiece enlarges the appearance of the sample 5 or 10 times). You may even have a view screen or an attached projector that acts as an ocular lens.

B. The **body tube** holds the ocular lens in position over the revolving nosepiece and the objective lenses (see below). The straight tube can be vertical or angled.

C. The **arm** is a curved metal piece that connects the body tube to the base and supports the stage.

D. The **revolving nosepiece** holds the objective lenses and allows you to change objective lenses when looking at a slide.

E. The **objective lenses**, or **objectives**, are the parts at the bottom of the body tube closest to the sample you are examining. Each objective has a lens and a tubelike holder. Like eyepieces, objectives come in various powers. The longer lenses allow for greater magnification of the image and are called high-power objectives. The shorter lenses have less magnification power and are called low-power objectives. The objective lenses can be labeled differently as well. Some microscopes have several objective lenses, for example, 4x, 10x, 40x, and 100x; some have only 1 or 2 objective lenses.

F. The **stage** is the flat surface on which you place your slides or samples. There is a hole in the center of the stage to allow light to pass from the light source up to the specimen.

G. The **stage clips** hold the slide in place on the stage. Some microscopes have a movable stage, and the slides are held in place by movable jaws.

H. The **disc diaphragm** is used to adjust the amount of light shining through the sample on the stage. (Some microscopes do not have diaphragms.) When the diaphragm opening is reduced, less light will pass toward the specimen and the image will appear darker.

I. The **coarse-adjustment knob** is the large knob used to adjust the position of the body tube, allowing you to quickly bring your sample into view. The coarse-adjustment knob should not be used when focusing under the higher-power objectives.

J. The **fine-adjustment knob** is the small knob used to change the position of the body tube, allowing you to make small adjustments to the focus of your sample. Most microscopes have both coarse- and fine-adjustment knobs, but some have only one knob.

K. Your microscope is illuminated by a **mirror**, or **lamp**, located beneath the diaphragm. This increases the amount of light shining through your sample. If your microscope has a lamp, it may be battery-powered or have a cord that plugs into an electrical outlet.

L. The **base** of the microscope is the heavy bottom part. It supports all the other parts of the microscope.

Magnification

Notations on your microscope's lenses tell you how many times bigger than normal the lenses make the samples appear. To calculate the magnification of the things you are looking at, you need to look at both the ocular and the objective lenses. If the ocular lens in your eyepiece bears the notation 10x, that means if it were used on its own, the objects you view through it would appear to be 10 times larger than they actually are. If you use this ocular lens with your low-power objective, which bears the notation 4x, then the total magnification of the object can be calculated by multiplying the magnification powers of the lenses together—in this case the total magnification is 40x. If you use the same ocular lens with a 10x magnification, a 10x objective lens would make objects appear 10 times 10, or 100 times bigger than they actually are, and a 40x objective lens would magnify objects 400 times.

> To find the magnification, take the number written on the side of your ocular lens and multiply it by the number written on the side of the objective lens.

Note: The number of times an image in this book has been magnified is indicated in the caption below the photomicrograph. However, these images may have been cropped in the production process (only a portion of the image has been used), and/or then resized for printing.

Sugar Crystal x100.

Resolution

While you may think that the most important thing to consider about a microscope is the magnification, what you really should be looking at is the **resolution**.

Resolution is the ability to see objects that are small and close together as separate objects. Without a microscope you can tell the difference between two objects that are about 0.3 millimeters (mm) apart, but with a microscope you can tell the difference between two objects that are 0.0003 mm apart, or about 1,000 times better resolution. But magnifying an object by 1,000 times is about as good as light microscopes get. To resolve even smaller objects, you need to use a different kind of microscope. Scientists generally use powerful **electron microscopes** for these kinds of samples (see page 87). Now that you know the different parts of the microscope and how to use them, you can begin exploring the microscopic world.

Bringing It into Focus

You're probably anxious to get started using your microscope. There are a few simple rules that you should follow to avoid damaging your microscope or your slides.

Focusing

1. Remove your microscope from its box or cover. Always pick up your microscope correctly by grasping it firmly with two hands, one hand under the base and the other on the arm. Be careful with microscopes that have lamps attached near the base. Lamps may become hot after use, so let lamps cool before carrying the microscope, and support it by the base to prevent burning your hand.

2. Place the microscope on a table, away from the edge. Move it to a position so that you can look through the ocular lens comfortably. Use a chair or a stool if you find that more comfortable than standing.

3. Make sure the low-power objective lens is in place over the hole in the stage. Use the coarse-adjustment knob to raise the objective lenses so they are about 1 inch (2.5 centimeters [cm]) above the stage.

4. Place your sample on the stage, carefully using the stage clips to secure it. Do not snap the stage clips, as you could damage the clips or the sample. Adjust the position of your sample so that it is over the hole in the stage.

5. Adjust your mirror to focus light through the diaphragm. You should be able to see a circle of light when you look into the eyepiece. If you do not see a circle of light, but only a partial circle, check to make sure the objective lens is in its correct position, aligned with the body tube. Never use your microscope in direct sunlight, as the reflected light could damage your eyes. If your microscope has a lamp, turn it on. You may need to replace the batteries or plug it into an electrical outlet, depending on the style of microscope you have. When viewing very thick samples, you may have to shine light on the sample from above. You can do this by using a table lamp or by placing your microscope in a brightly lit place.

6. Look at the objective lens from the side and use the coarse-adjustment knob to lower the lens as close as possible to the sample.

7. Look through the eyepiece and use the coarse-adjustment knob to move the lens away from the sample. This process, called **focusing upward**, should bring the sample into view. If you go too far, simply begin again at step 6.

8. When the sample is in view, use the fine-adjustment knob to clearly focus your sample. Slide the sample gently sideways to bring it into the center of your **field of view** (the area visible through the lens of an optical instrument).

9. When you wish to use the high-power objective lens, simply turn the revolving nosepiece to bring the high-power lens into position over your sample. You should be able to see the sample through the high-power objective, so you will have to adjust only the fine-adjustment knob. Remember to always focus upward so that the lens is moving away from the sample. Focusing downward could break your slide or damage your lenses.

10. Always return to the low-power objective before removing the sample from the stage. It will be easier to get the slide out, and you might scratch the lenses if you don't, as the high-power objective will be closer to the slide. To look at another sample, repeat steps 3 through 9.

11. When you are finished using your microscope, make sure the low-power objective is in position over the hole in the stage. Be sure to turn off the light.

12. If your lenses get dirty, you may see spots or smudges when you look through the microscope, even if no sample is present. To clean the lenses, always use lens paper, which you can purchase at any camera store. Tissue paper or cloth could damage your lenses. Breathe onto the surface of the lens and wipe in a circular motion.

13. Be sure to store your microscope covered, using a box or bag (use a plastic grocery bag if necessary). If your microscope has batteries, you should remove the batteries when you store the microscope for extended periods, as batteries might corrode and damage the casing. Store your microscope someplace where it won't get wet or bumped. Make sure you support the box or bag when moving the microscope.

Troubleshooting

When I look through my light microscope at a sample, it looks like the one in the book, but it is a different color.
Taking photomicrographs is a tricky procedure. Different microscopy techniques, as well as the cameras and computer programs we used to create the photomicrographs in this book, can affect the characteristics of the specimen (for example, the color), so the photomicrographs shown here may not match perfectly the specimens you see through your microscope. We tried as much as possible to match the colors we were seeing through the lenses to the ones produced on the computer screen, but we may not have been able to achieve a perfect match. The color you see is affected by the amount of light on the sample. If you adjust your microscope's light source and diaphragm (if your microscope has one), you may see the sample color change with the amount of light.

When I look through my light microscope, I get only a dark outline of my sample. I cannot see any detail.
Hold your slide up to a light. If you cannot see through the sample, then your sample is too thick. Try making another sample, but slice it thinner. You may need an adult's help, as you must use a very sharp blade. If you think you have the thinnest sample possible, try increasing the light going through the sample, if it is possible to do that on your microscope. Or you could shine light on the sample from the side or above, and just view the surface of your sample, as is done with a dissecting microscope.

When I look through my microscope, I can't find my sample on the slide.
Always start looking for your sample using the lowest-power objective lens. Find an edge of the slide closest to the sample; then slowly move the slide toward the area where the light is shining the brightest. Focus each time you move the slide. You will have to practice, as the fine movements necessary to get the sample in focus take time to learn.

Magnification—Units of Measurement: How Big Is It?

When you view a sample under the microscope, it may be difficult to judge what size it is. What was just a tiny speck now takes up the entire **field of view**. A **stage micrometer** is a slide equipped with a measuring scale, which allows you to measure very small objects. If your microscope came equipped with a stage micrometer, you can follow the directions below to use it. The best stage micrometers have lines that are very clear under the high-power objective; they can be quite expensive because they are difficult to make. If you don't have a stage micrometer, you still can make rough measurements using your microscope and a clear, thin plastic ruler.

You Will Need

Microscope
Micrometer slide or clear, thin plastic ruler
Paper
Pen or pencil

What to Do

1. Place the micrometer slide or clear plastic ruler on the stage of your microscope and secure it with the stage clips.
2. Look at the slide or ruler under the low-power objective. Move the slide or ruler so that it lies across the longest part of the field of view. This is the **field diameter**. Count the number of millimeter divisions you can see. Write this number down. Use this number when measuring samples viewed under the low-power objective.
3. Look at the slide or ruler under the high-power objective, and count the number of millimeters across the diameter. Write down this number. This is the number you will use when measuring samples viewed under the high-power objective.

Relic Hunter

Treasure seekers roam the world looking for artifacts, or objects made by people of past civilizations. If these relic hunters used only a microscope, they wouldn't have to leave the comfort of their own homes. Microscope artifacts are objects accidentally created when a microscope slide is made. The most common type of artifact people make when creating light-microscope slides with water is an air bubble, but an artifact can be any type of object that is not naturally part of your sample.

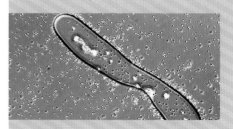

Bubbles in cream x50.

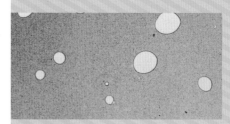

Bubbles in Potato Starch x100.

Bubbles in skim milk x50.

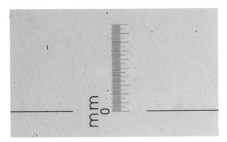

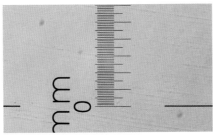

Stage micrometer x50. The lines are 0.01 mm apart.

Stage micrometer x100.

Stage micrometer x200.

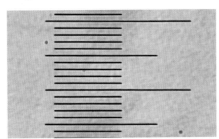

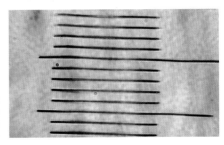

Stage micrometer x400.

Stage micrometer x630.

4. Place the sample slide that you wish to measure on the stage of your microscope and secure it with the stage clips. Look at the sample first with the low-power objective. Move the sample so it stretches across the center of the field of view. How much of the field of view does the sample cover or stretch across? For example, if the number of millimeter divisions you can see on your low-power objective is 20 and your sample covers half the space, then your sample stretches 10 millimeters. If the sample covers roughly one quarter of the space, then it is about 5 millimeters.

5. If the sample covers only a very small portion of the field of view, try looking at it using the high-power objective. If you are measuring your sample under the high-power objective, be sure to use the high-power field diameter measurements.

6. If your microscope has a scale or micrometer built into the eyepiece, you can use it to measure your samples. You will still need the micrometer slide to measure the markings on the micrometer eyepiece. These markings have different values for the high- and low-power objective lenses. Instead of measuring the diameter of the field of view, measure the distance from one end of the scale to the other.

Floaters—What's That in My Eye?

Sometimes when you look through a microscope you see tiny floating objects that are not part of your sample at all—they are part of your eye! These small spots are caused by strands of material inside your eyeball and they are called **floaters** because what you see looks like objects floating past your eye. They are a normal part of your eye, so you don't have to worry about seeing them. If you see something moving across the field of view of your microscope, and it doesn't change when you adjust the magnification, it might just be a floater.

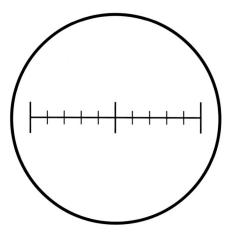

Micrometer eyepiece.

Drawing

If you don't have a digital or film camera to attach to your microscope, don't worry. Long before cameras, scientists used paper and pencils to draw what they saw through their lenses. Just use a pencil and compass or jar lid to draw a circle about 4 inches (10 cm) in diameter on unlined, white paper. This will represent your field of view. To draw what you see through the microscope, look through the eyepiece with one eye and look at the paper with the other eye. It may take you a while to be comfortable doing this, so practice a lot! Try to make your drawing as clear as possible. Your drawings will be more realistic if you draw them in the correct colors. Label your drawings. Include the magnification you are using. You may wish to include the sizes of any objects you have measured using the steps in the "Magnification—Units of Measurement: How Big Is It?" procedure, or the size of the field of view. Now you can paste or tape your drawing onto your notebook page or recipe card.

Microscopists look at objects that are very, very tiny. Like other scientists, they use a system of measurement known as the **International System of Units**, or SI (from the French *Système International d'Unités*), based on the **metric system**. The metric system uses multiples of 10 and is based on a standard length of 1 meter. Microscope objects are usually measured in either millimeters (mm) or micrometers (µm), also called microns. A millimeter is 1/1,000 of a meter. A micrometer is 1/1,000 of a millimeter. Some metric units that we need are given here, as well as some conversion to metric units from the customary, or standard, units used in the United States (see also page 133). The U.S. customary units were based on a collection of English units called the Imperial system that no longer is used in most countries and now is defined in England entirely in terms of metric equivalents.

Metric Units

1 meter (m) = 100 centimeters (cm)

1 meter = 1,000 millimeters (mm)

1 meter = 1,000,000 micrometers (µm)

1 centimeter = 10 millimeters

1 centimeter = 10,000 micrometers

1 millimeter = 1,000 micrometers

From U.S. Customary to Metric Units

1 yard = 0.915 meter (m)

1 foot = 30.48 centimeters (cm)

1 inch = 2.54 centimeters (cm)

Keeping a Journal

Scientists write down information about their experiments so they know what they did and what happened as a result. When you look at samples with your microscope, keep a record of your work in a notebook or on large index or recipe cards. Using a computer, it is simple to create your own personal journal. If you have the type of microscope that takes photomicrographs, you might want to attach an image of your sample to each journal page.

DATE SAMPLE GATHERED: DATE OF SLIDE:

WHAT SAMPLE IS: WHERE SAMPLE IS FROM:

HOW SAMPLE WAS PREPARED:

METHOD:

STAINS:

MOUNT:

OBJECTIVE/LENS USED:

LIGHTING USED:

OBSERVATIONS:

ESTIMATED SIZE OF SAMPLE:

DRAWING OF SAMPLE:

Part 1
Microscopes and Slides
Chapter 3
Different Kinds of Slides and When to Use Them

A word of advice before you begin making slides: Have all the materials you need handy, and make certain that an adult handles all sharp objects. Sample materials sometimes have a short life span. Wet mounted slides will dry out if you leave them on the counter overnight. Slides are best viewed immediately after you have prepared them, so don't make too many prepared specimens ahead of time in the hopes of looking at them later.

Wet Mounts

Wet mounts include hair, **cork**, and thin sections of plant materials.

You Will Need

Eyedropper

Water

Slide

Tweezers

Your sample

Coverslip

Tissue or paper towel

Petroleum jelly (optional)

What to Do

1. Use an eyedropper to place a drop of water on the slide.
2. Use tweezers to place the object on top of the water droplet.
3. Hold the coverslip upright at a 45-degree angle so that one edge of the slip touches the edge of the drop of water.
4. Gently lower the coverslip over the drop of water and sample, trying not to trap any air bubbles (see the sidebar "Relic Hunter" on artifacts, page 22).
5. Blot up excess water with a tissue or paper towel.
6. If your slide begins to dry out while you are looking at it, place a drop of water next to the coverslip on a side that still seems wet. The water will move under the coverslip and push out any air bubbles.
7. If you are going to be viewing a wet mount for a long period of time, use a toothpick to put a thin seal of petroleum jelly around the outside of the coverslip. This will prevent evaporation.

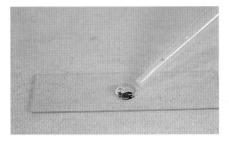

Placing a drop of water on the slide. Photo courtesy El'ad Tzadok.

The coverslip is held at a 45-degree angle to allow one edge to touch the drop of water before the slip is gently lowered over the drop. Photo courtesy El'ad Tzadok.

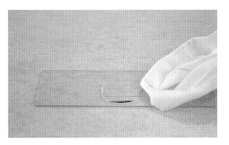

Blotting up excess water with a tissue. Photo courtesy El'ad Tzadok.

Smear Slide

A typical sample for which a smear slide is used is yogurt. In general, use this type of slide for liquid samples.

You Will Need

Eyedropper or toothpick
Two slides
Coverslip
Tissue or paper towel

What to Do

1. Use an eyedropper or toothpick to place a small drop of the sample on one end of a clean slide.
2. Drag the edge of another clean slide across the liquid to spread a thin layer over the surface of the bottom slide.
3. Hold the coverslip upright at a 45-degree angle so that one edge of the slip touches the edge of the smear.
4. Gently lower the coverslip over the smear, trying not to trap any air bubbles.
5. Blot up excess liquid with a tissue or paper towel.

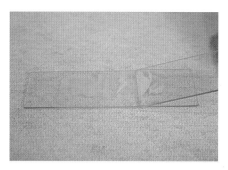

Dragging the edge of another clean slide across the liquid to spread a thin layer. Photo courtesy El'ad Tzadok.

The coverslip lowered over the smear. Photo courtesy El'ad Tzadok.

Well Slide

A well slide is useful for looking at specimens living in liquids such as pond water. You can buy well slides already made or you can make your own.

You Will Need

Slide
Paper towels
Toothpick
Clear nail polish
Eyedropper
Coverslip

What to Do

1. Place a slide on a clean paper towel on a flat surface.
2. In the center of the slide, use a toothpick to draw a circle with the nail polish (about ½ inch (1 cm) in diameter). Allow the nail polish to dry.
3. Add several additional layers of nail polish, allowing the nail polish to dry completely between each layer. This process creates a well on the slide.
4. Place your sample in the well and use an eyedropper to add enough water to fill the well. Gently place a coverslip on top, being careful not to trap any air bubbles. Blot up any excess liquid with a paper towel.

Caution: Well slides are thicker than regular slides, so use care when focusing so you don't damage the slide or your lenses. You may not be able to focus using the larger magnifying objectives because the slide is too thick.

Using a toothpick to draw a circle with the nail polish. We used colored nail polish for the photo since clear nail polish is almost invisible. Photo courtesy El'ad Tzadok.

Pulling a Stain

Pulling a stain lets you stain or color a specimen—for example, onion skin, which is the very thin tissue of cells that lines the outer and inner surfaces of an onion layer—that is already placed on a slide.

You Will Need

Eyedropper
Stain, such as tincture of iodine
Prepared wet-mount slide
Coverslip
Tissue or paper towel

What to Do

1. Prepare a wet mount of the specimen (onion skin) using water as noted above.
2. Use an eyedropper to place a drop of stain on the slide next to the coverslip.
3. Carefully touch a piece of tissue or paper towel to the side of the coverslip opposite to the drop of stain.
4. The tissue or paper towel will become damp and the drop of stain will move through the sample.
5. Add more stain until the stain begins to show on the tissue or paper towel. Carefully blot up any extra stain from the sides of the coverslip.

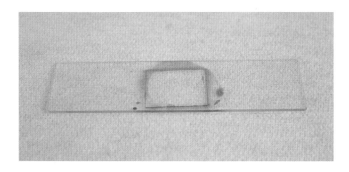

Stain placed with an eyedropper on the slide next to the coverslip. Photo courtesy El'ad Tzadok.

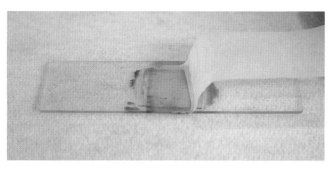

Using tissue to draw the stain through the sample. Photo courtesy El'ad Tzadok.

Squash Slide

The squash slide is the technique to use with very soft samples, such as an onion root tip.

You Will Need

Eyedropper
Water
Slide
Tweezers
Coverslip
Lens paper
Petroleum jelly

What to Do

1. Use an eyedropper to place a drop of water in the middle of the slide. Place your sample in the water droplet using tweezers.
2. Put the coverslip on top of the sample and cover it with a piece of lens paper.
3. Gently press down on the paper, being careful not to break the coverslip. You should feel the sample being squashed flat.
4. Remove the lens paper and look at the sample. If it looks too thick for viewing through the microscope, try pressing down on it again. When you are satisfied that your sample is thin enough to view through your microscope, place a thin layer of petroleum jelly around the edge of the coverslip to keep the sample from drying out.

Sample placed in the water droplet.
Photo courtesy El'ad Tzadok.

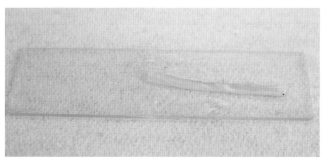

Check whether the sample looks thin enough to view through your microscope. Photo courtesy El'ad Tzadok.

Acetate Peel

When you have a sample with an interesting surface, such as a coin, the acetate peel technique works very well.

> *Caution:* Check with an adult before using this technique on any object. Acetone can damage varnished, painted, or finished wood surfaces.

You Will Need

Nail polish remover containing acetone

Cotton ball

Either an acetate sheet like the type used for overhead projectors or a piece of cellophane tape

Soap and water

Tweezers

Scissors

What to Do

1. Pour some nail polish remover onto a cotton ball.
2. Wet the surface of the item you wish to observe with the cotton ball. Any item with a dry, rough, or textured surface work wells. Do not use this technique on any varnished, painted, or finished wood surfaces.
3. Press the wet surface of the item into the acetate sheet.
4. Leave the item on the acetate sheet for several minutes to allow the print to set.
5. Carefully peel or pull the sheet away from the item. Clean the item well with soap and water.
6. Hold the acetate with tweezers and use scissors to cut a sample to fit onto the center of a slide.
7. Using the tweezers, place the trimmed acetate print onto the slide.
8. Place the slide on the stage of the microscope and secure it with the stage clips.
9. Examine your slide under the low-power objective.

Leave the item for several minutes so the print on the acetate (or cellophane tape) can set. Photo courtesy El'ad Tzadok.

Rice Infusion

An easy way to corral small critters, for example, pond or sea life, onto a slide is by using a rice infusion.

You Will Need

Shallow bowl
Slide
Several grains of uncooked rice
Coverslip
Tissue or lens paper

What to Do

1. Place the seawater or pond water you have collected in a shallow bowl.
2. Drop a slide into the bowl and gently shake the bowl back and forth.
3. Place several grains of rice into the water and leave the bowl undisturbed on a counter overnight (you can cover the bowl, but air should still be able to get in and out). When you are ready to view the slide, carefully lift the slide from the bowl, trying not to pour off the slime or material on the surface of the slide.
4. Place a coverslip over the center of the slide and use a tissue or lens paper to wipe off the excess water off the slide before viewing.

Drop the slide in the bowl of seawater or pond water and add several grains of rice. Photo courtesy El'ad Tzadok.

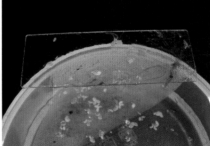

Carefully lift the slide out, trying not to pour off the material on its surface. Photo courtesy El'ad Tzadok.

Permanent Mounts

The **permanent mount** is the technique to use if you want to keep your slides for several days. It works best with samples that don't contain water, such as hair or fibers.

You Will Need

Colorless nail polish
Slide
Tweezers
Coverslip

What to Do

1. Place a drop of clear nail polish on the center of the slide.
2. Gently place your sample onto the drop of nail polish using tweezers.
3. Hold the coverslip upright so that one edge of the slip touches the edge of the drop of nail polish.
4. Gently lower the coverslip over the drop of polish and sample, trying not to trap any air bubbles.

Use tweezers to gently place the sample in the clear nail polish on the center of the slide. Photo courtesy El'ad Tzadok.

Trapping Living Things

If your samples contain small living things, such as pond creatures that move too fast for you to see, here is a way to slow them down so you can see them.

1. Pull several strands from a cotton ball and place them in the center of the slide.
2. With an eyedropper, transfer a drop or two of the water that contains your creatures on top of the cotton strands.
3. Gently place the coverslip on top of the water and cotton strand sample. Do not press down.
4. Place the slide on the stage of the microscope and secure it with the stage clips.
5. Look at your slide using the low-power objective. You may have to reduce the amount of light going through the diaphragm to see the pond creatures more easily. Move the slide around gently to see more of them.
6. When you have found some, place them in the center of your field of view and look at them with the high-power objective.

If the cotton strands don't work, you can also try adding a drop of white corn syrup to the slide to slow down your creatures.

Placing strands from a cotton ball in the center of the slide to slow down living creatures. Photo courtesy El'ad Tzadok.

Part 2

Getting Started

Chapter 4

First Experiments

Making a Microtome

The **microtome** is a piece of equipment that helps you cut very thin slices or sections of samples. A very thin section allows light through so you can see the sample's structure easily. Here's how to make your own simple microtome.

You Will Need

Wooden or plastic spool from thread

Flat-head metal bolt that just fits through the hole in the spool

Metal nut that fits the bolt

Waterproof glue

Popsicle stick

Fine-point waterproof marker

Piece of carrot

Knife or single-edged razor blade (to be handled by an adult only) ◣

Bowl of water

Tweezers

Microscope slide and coverslip

What to Do

1. Thread the bolt through the nut and screw it into the spool to make sure it fits. Then remove the bolt and have an adult attach the nut to the spool using waterproof glue. Allow the glue to set.

2. Have an adult glue the head of the bolt to the middle of the flat side of a Popsicle stick. Allow the glue to set. The Popsicle stick acts as your handle.

3. Screw the metal bolt through the nut so it extends up into the spool. Do not tighten the bolt. Thread it on, leaving a space inside the spool for your sample.

4. Use a fine-point waterproof marker to draw an X and then another X on the bottom of the spool. This will create eight equally spaced lines around the bottom of the spool. These will help you turn the handle on the bolt the same amount to make each section the same thickness. You are now ready to use your microtome.

5. When the bolt is not fully screwed into the nut, there will be a space at the top of the spool where the specimen fits. Have an adult cut your sample to fit inside this space at the top of the spool. A piece of carrot can be used to fill in any empty spaces or support oddly shaped samples.

6. Have an adult slice across the top of your sample with a knife or single-edged razor blade. Dip the blade and the section into a bowl of water. The section should float off of the blade. Turn the handle and cut another section. Repeat the dipping and cutting process until you have several sections.

7. Use tweezers to transfer your sections to slides. Make a wet mount, following the directions on page 27.

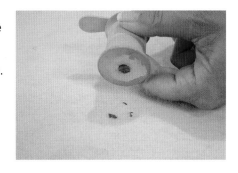

The bolt with the handle screws through the nut glued to the spool. The bolt is inserted into the center of the spool. The gap in the center of the spool is filled with the sample so it can be sliced into thin sections.

This Experiment Is Brought to You by the Letter E

If you think you know what the letter e looks like, think again. When you examine your sample under a microscope, you'll be very surprised to discover the changes lenses can make to the printed letter. This experiment will also give you lots of practice moving things into (and out of) the field of view.

You Will Need

Method 1
Page of newspaper
Ruler

Method 2
Page of newspaper
Ruler
Scissors
Transparent cellophane tape
Slides

What to Do

Method 1

1. Find a section of print on the newspaper that contains a small letter e. Tear out a 2-inch by 3-inch (5-cm by 7.5-cm) piece of the newspaper.
2. Place the strip of paper on the stage of your microscope. Position it so that the letter e is directly under the low-power objective lens. Secure the paper with the stage clips.
3. Make sure your microscope is in a brightly lit area, or use a table lamp to shine light onto the top of the newspaper.
4. Carefully focus the microscope so that you can clearly see the letter e. Compare the e you see with your naked eye to the e you see with the microscope.
5. Look through the eyepiece while moving the paper in different directions—back and forth, side to side. Notice which way the magnified image moves.
6. Try this with other letters. Look for the letters a, f, h, and r.
7. Move the newspaper so that the torn edge is directly under the low-power objective lens. Refocus the microscope if necessary. Look at the **fibers** that make up the paper.

Method 2

1. Find a section of print on the newspaper that contains the letter e. Cut the letter e out of the newspaper.
2. Cellophane tape the letter directly to a slide.
3. Place the slide on the stage of the microscope and secure it with the stage clips.
4. Make sure your microscope is in a brightly lit area, or use a table lamp to shine light onto the top of the newspaper.
5. Carefully focus the microscope so that you can clearly see the letter e. Compare the e you see with your naked eye to the e you see with the microscope.
6. Look through the eyepiece while moving the slide in different directions—back and forth, side to side. Notice which way the magnified image moves.
7. Try this with other letters. Look for the letters a, f, h, and r.

Letter e x12.

Letter e x25.

What Did You See?

Not only were the letters bigger when you looked at them through the microscope, but they also were upside down and backward. You probably noticed another strange thing: the movement was also backward. When you moved the paper to the right, the viewed image in the microscope moved to the left. When you moved the paper toward you, the image in the microscope moved away from you. This is often confusing (and irritating) for new microscope users, because whenever they try to move the sample to the left it goes right! It does get easier with practice. The lenses inside the microscope bend the light so that the image you see is the reverse of the object you are looking at.

When you focused on the edges of the paper, you could see the wood fibers from which the paper was made. The fibers even faced the same direction. This is called the **grain** of the paper and it is what holds the paper together.

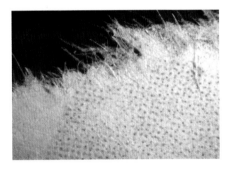

Edge of newspaper x12.

Edge of newspaper x25.

Even without using a microscope, you can see the tiny fibers that make up newsprint. Tear a piece of newspaper and look closely at the edge. These rough fibers or threadlike pieces of wood pulp are what hold the paper together. Paper can be made from any type of plant material because plants contain the fiber-making chemical cellulose. When cellulose and water are mixed together during papermaking, the cellulose fibers get bonded together, and when the mixture dries, you get paper.

Comic Strips

Grab your favorite comic book or the color comics from the weekend paper for this experiment. Learn something new about microscopes and newspapers at the same time.

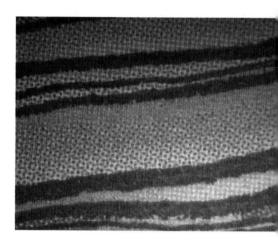

You Will Need

Microscope
Color comic book or color comic section of newspaper
Reading lamp
Paper
Pen or pencil

What to Do

1. Find a picture in the color comics that is orange, green, flesh colored, or purple. The picture should be large enough to cover the hole in your microscope stage.
2. Cut a 1-inch by 3-inch (2.5-cm by 7.5-cm) strip of the paper with the picture you have chosen in the center of it.
3. Place the strip on the stage of the microscope and secure it with the stage clips.
4. Shine light onto the top of the paper using the reading lamp.
5. Bring the sample into focus with the low-power objective, following the steps on page 19–20.
6. Count the number of dots of one of the colors that you can see and record this number.
7. Change to the high-power objective and count the number of dots in the same color and compare this with the number you recorded in step 6.

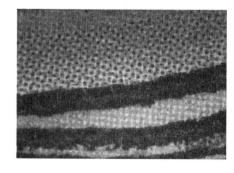

Comic strip x 12.

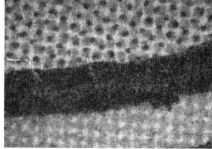

Comic strip x 25.

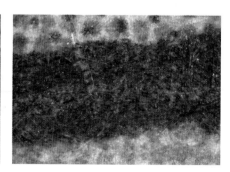

Comic strip x 50.

What Did You See?

You were probably surprised to discover that there were different-color dots that made up the solid-color pictures of the comics. Newspaper pictures are made with about 60 dots per inch (24 dots per cm). Printed pictures in magazines and books are made with as many as 400 dots per inch (160 dots per cm). Your brain blends the different dots together to form the colors you see.

Another strange thing was the fact that you could see more dots through the low-power lens than through the high-power lens. The area that you see through the microscope is called the field of view.

When you switch from the low-power to the high-power objective, the objects appear to be larger, but you see fewer of them because as the field is magnified, you are viewing less of it. To better understand this, you could compare the field of vision to a dinner plate. Under the low-power objective, the dots are small, like marbles. Under the high-power objective, they appear to be large, like soccer balls. How many marbles do you think you could place next to each other on a dinner plate? How many soccer balls? Try it and see!

Sew Long—Depth of Field

Have you ever tried to take a photograph of something or someone standing in front of a background of trees, a distant mountain, or an object? You may have noticed that either the subject or the background will be in focus, but you can't seem to get them both in focus. This is because your camera is unable to get both images to focus sharply at the same time. The same thing happens with your microscope. Now that you have had a chance to view something with your microscope, you probably noticed that not everything you can see is in focus (or sharp) at the same time. As you focus on one area, another area seems to become fuzzy or unclear. This problem only gets worse when you use a higher magnification or objective. Just in case you haven't noticed this, here's an experiment to show you what happens.

You Will Need

Slide

Clear nail polish or water

Tweezers

3½-inch (1 cm) pieces of
sewing thread in different
colors (e.g., yellow, red,
and blue)

Coverslip

What to Do

1. Place a slide on a clean paper towel on a flat surface.
2. Place a drop of clear, colorless nail polish in the center of the slide. This will create a permanent slide. If you don't have nail polish, you can use water to create a temporary slide.
3. With the tweezers, place a piece of sewing thread into the center of the nail polish so that it is parallel to the long side of the slide.
4. With the tweezers, place a second piece of sewing thread of a different color across the top of the first piece of thread at a 45-degree angle to form an X shape.
5. Carefully place a third piece of thread of a third color across the top of the first two pieces of thread. This one should be at an angle so that the bottom pieces of thread can still be seen.
6. Hold the coverslip upright so that one edge of the slip touches the edge of the drop of nail polish.
7. Gently lower the coverslip over the three pieces of thread, trying not to trap any air bubbles.
8. Place the slide on the stage of the microscope and secure it with the stage clips.
9. Look at your slide with the microscope using the low-power objective. Place the point at which the three threads cross in the center of your field of view. Focus on each of the three threads.
10. Repeat this process using the high-power objective. Again focus on each of the three threads.

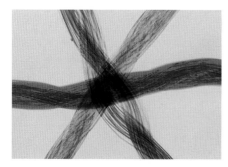

Threads x50.

Threads x100.

Threads x200.

What Did You See?

When you looked at your slide using the low-power objective lens, you were able to see all three threads pretty clearly. You might have had to use the fine-adjustment knob a little bit to make each one a bit clearer. When you switched to the high-power objective lens, it became more difficult to focus on more than one of the threads at a time. This is because of a change in the depth of field as you switched from the low-power objective to the high-power objective. The high-power objective bends the light more, so it has a narrower range of focus than the low-power objective. When you are preparing samples for higher magnifications, you must ensure that they are very thin so that all areas of the sample can be in focus at the same time.

Oil Immersion Lens

Some microscopes have a special type of lens called an **oil immersion lens**. This lens is used by placing a drop of oil on the top of the coverslip and adjusting the position of the lens so that it is touching the drop of oil. The oil bends the light more than the air would, so more light can enter the microscope. Oil immersion lenses make it easier to see samples because they increase the amount of light going through the sample and the microscope and into your eye.

Part 3
Activities
Chapter 5
Crime Scene or "Crime Seen"?

Criminals always leave something behind at the scene of a crime. Even though they may wear gloves, masks, or even special clothing, microscopic evidence still can be found. Here are some of the things that law enforcement agencies look for when examining the scene of a crime.

Prints Charming

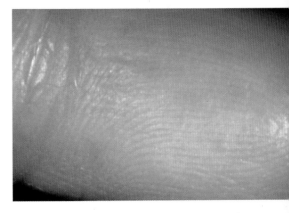

No two people have been found to have the same fingerprint, not even identical twins. Police can compare a print they have found at a crime scene with other prints they have on file in their computers. They can also compare this print with a suspect's to determine whether there is a match. Fingerprints have been used as a way of identifying criminals for more than a century. Here are two ways of making fingerprints and studying them.

Finger with characteristic swirl pattern x6.

You Will Need

Method 1
Washable-ink stamp pad
White paper or card
Soap and water
Magnifying glass
Notebook
Scissors
Pen

Method 2
Cocoa powder
Clear cellophane tape
Slide
Tweezers
Small clean paintbrush or
   makeup brush

Fingerprint taken using an ink pad x6.

What to Do

Method 1: Fingerprinting

1. Roll your finger from side to side on a washable-ink stamp pad.
2. Carefully roll your finger across a piece of white paper or a card. Roll it in only one direction to keep from smudging the fingerprint.
3. Lift your finger off the paper and immediately wash your hands with soap and water. This will keep the surfaces of the table, microscope, and especially the walls of your house clean!
4. View the print using a magnifying glass. See what patterns you can recognize.
5. Use the scissors to cut out the section of the paper containing the print and place the print on the stage of the microscope, securing it with the stage clips. Shine a light on your sample from the top. Examine your print under the low-power objective. What patterns can you see now?
6. Keep a record, noting the name of the person who the fingerprint belongs to, which fingers were sampled, and the age of the person.

Method 2: Dusting for Prints

1. Look around your house for fingerprints. If you have a younger brother or sister, their fingerprints are probably all over everything. Smooth surfaces such as polished tables, doorknobs, and mirrors are good places to look. Ask an adult's permission before performing the next step.

2. Dip a brush into the cocoa, and shake off the excess powder. Use this to sprinkle a small amount of cocoa powder on the fingerprint. Gently blow away the loose powder. The fingerprint should be clearly visible.

3. Tear off a piece of cellophane tape slightly larger than the fingerprint.

4. Hold one end of the tape and press the rest of the tape over the fingerprint. Use the side of your finger to rub the tape back and forth in order to transfer the print.

5. Lift the tape with the tweezers and place it on the center of a slide.

6. Place the slide on the stage of the microscope and secure it with the stage clips.

7. Examine your slide under the low-power objective. Can you figure out who the print belongs to?

 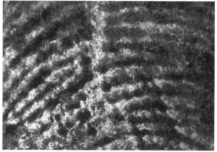

Fingerprint taken using cocoa powder x6.   Fingerprint taken using cocoa powder x12.

What Did You See?

In each of the methods above, you made a fingerprint. In the first method, the ink covered the ridges (parts of the fingerprint that were raised), while leaving the furrows (the deeper parts of the fingerprint) without much ink. This means that the different parts of the finger have different amounts of ink on them. When the inked finger was rolled on the paper, the ridges, which were more heavily inked, left a print.

In the second method, the cocoa powder acted like the ink and attached itself to the print. The cellophane tape lifted the cocoa powder and formed the impression of the print.

Fingerprint Features

Fingerprint analysts use tiny differences between fingerprints to make matches between samples. In addition to the shapes of the ridges that make up the print, analysts use points of comparison, which are the spots where the ridges split or end.

Here are some of the different fingerprint features that experts use to help identify prints.

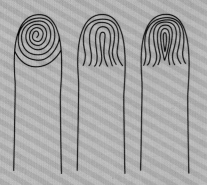

Whorl   Loop   Island

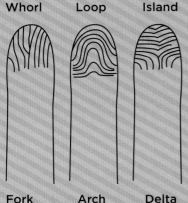

Fork   Arch   Delta

Did You Know?

In addition to fingertips, other body parts have patterns that can be used for matching people to prints. You can use the palms of the hands, soles of the feet, or toes, but you can't use noses because they have no ridges.

Fiber Optics

If you've ever worn a wool sweater, you may have found fibers or bits of material in your hair, on your jacket, or covering your pants. Clothing has a funny way of unraveling. Threads found at a crime scene can tell police something about what the suspect was wearing at the time of the crime.

You Will Need

Piece of thread or cloth made from any of the following materials:
  silk, wool, cashmere, nylon, polyester, linen, cotton, mixed blends
  (or, you can use small loose fibers vacuumed from a carpet)
Scissors
Slides
Coverslips
Eyedropper
Water
Microscope
Pen
Paper

What to Do

1. Cut a small piece of thread. If you use cloth, look for any loose threads to use. Ask a parent to help you cut the thread.
2. Make a wet mount of the slide, following the instructions on page 27. Label the slide so that you know what thread you are looking at. Keep a record of what the materials look like.
3. Place the slide on the stage of the microscope and secure it with the stage clips.
4. Observe your slide using the low-power and high-power objectives.
5. Using your knowledge of fibers, see whether you can tell what fibers make up mixed blends.

Bamboo x50.

What Did You See?

Each fiber had its own distinct appearance. Wool, like the cashmere (goat hair wool) samples, looks broken or scaly. This is because wool comes from sheep and so more closely resembles animal hair. Threads made from plants also resemble one another. Cotton looks like a flattened tube or ribbon, while linen fiber looks like a rounded, thicker version of cotton. Silk is made from the thread of a silkworm. Silk fiber looks like a piece of glass; it is round, even, and solid. Synthetic threads are chemically produced and spun. They also tend to be smooth.

Cashmere x400.

Cotton x400.

Did You Know?

Nylon is a synthetic fiber that has been around since the 1930s. It was the first fiber to be made completely from petrochemicals (the stuff used to make gasoline) instead of natural plant or animal materials. The makers of nylon did take one lesson from nature: to make the fibers: they pushed the melted nylon through tiny holes called **spinerets** in the same way that silkworms push silk through their spinerets.

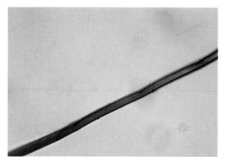

Silk x400.

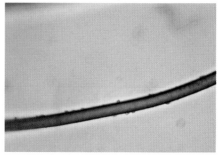

Polyester x400.

Hair Raising

Hair covers just about every inch of your body; it also falls off everyplace it is growing. Police scientists can tell whether a hair is dyed or bleached, can determine what part of the body the hair is from, and can even extract **DNA** evidence from the sample. So, clean up some old hairbrushes and let's get started!

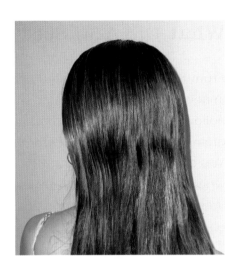

You Will Need

Hair from different family members or friends

Scissors

Slide

Water

Eyedropper

Coverslip

Tweezers

Tissue paper or paper towel

What to Do

1. Collect hair samples from family members or friends. You can gently pluck the hairs or you may wish to brush the hair and remove the hairs from the brush. Cut a ½-inch (1-cm) sample from each piece of hair you want to look at.
2. Make a wet mount of each hair sample following the steps on page 27. Label each slide so that you know which sample you are viewing.
3. Place the slide on the stage of the microscope and secure it with the stage clips.
4. Examine your slide under both the low-power and high-power objectives.
5. Look at the slides containing the other hair samples using the low-power and high-power objectives. Compare the different hair samples. You may wish to draw the different samples.

What Did You See?

From the samples illustrated here, you can see different parts of the hair shaft. Look closely at image A and you can see the outer scaly part, called the **cuticle**. The shaft of the hair, which is hollow, is like a long tube and is called the **cortex**. Inside the cortex is the **medulla**, which contains grains of pigment, or colored material. The hair in image B is from a woman who dyes her hair. You can see that the part of the hair closest to her scalp is completely white, and the hair is dark where the dye begins. This is because the medulla is full of air (not pigment), which makes the hair appear to be white. In general, brown hair tends to be thicker than blond, and blond hair tends to be thicker than red. Dyed hair has color not only in the medulla but also in the cortex and the cuticle.

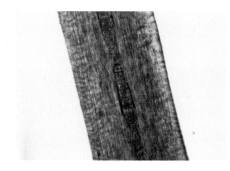

A: Brown hair x400 showing parts of hair shaft.

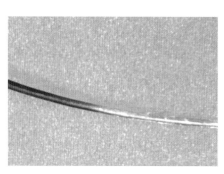

B: Gray hair under the dissecting microscope showing where the dye starts x25.

Blond hair x400.

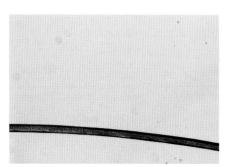

Red hair x50.

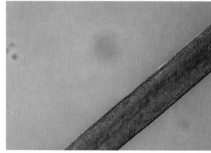

Red hair x200.

DNA

The **follicle**, or the part of the hair below your scalp, contains cells in which DNA can be found, so leaving even a single hair behind at the scene of a crime can tie you to the scene of a crime. **DNA**, or **deoxyribonucleic acid**, is a chemical found in every one of your cells. It contains your genetic code, the set of instructions your body uses to make new chemicals. Although most people have similar DNA, it turns out that there are small differences that, like fingerprints, can be used to identify individuals. Scientists need to use only a tiny amount of DNA to match people to samples found at crime scenes. Studies are also now being done to determine whether the DNA from plant samples can be used to match plant parts to individual trees or bushes.

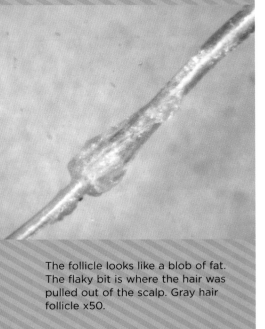

The follicle looks like a blob of fat. The flaky bit is where the hair was pulled out of the scalp. Gray hair follicle x50.

Don't Be Cheeky

Is there an easy and painless way to examine one of the cells in your body? Turns out that it's as simple as opening your mouth and saying, "Aaah." Let's see what's inside your cheek. ***Note:*** This is a good experiment to do at home, but check with your teacher before doing it at school. For health reasons, some schools don't allow any experiments that might involve working with saliva.

You Will Need

Wooden toothpick—the kind with a flat part on one end
Eyedropper
Water
Slide
Coverslip
Tincture of iodine
Tissue paper or lens paper
Soap and water

Caution: Use only your own cheek; do not use anyone else's.

What to Do

1. Use a new, clean wooden toothpick to gently scrape the inside lining of your cheek. You should not break the skin; just scrape the surface.
2. With an eyedropper, place two drops of water on a clean glass slide. Stir the toothpick back and forth in the water to transfer the cheek cells from the toothpick to the slide. This process will spread the cells out on the slide. Do not put the toothpick back into your mouth. Throw it away immediately.
3. Make a wet mount slide of this sample, following the instructions on page 27.

4. Place the slide on the stage of the microscope and secure it with the stage clips.

5. Observe your slide using the low- and high-power objectives.

6. When you have finished viewing the slide, place a drop of tincture of iodine next to the coverslip and use a piece of tissue paper or lens paper to pull the stain, following the instructions on page 30. Observe the slide again using the low- and high-power objectives. If there are many air bubbles in the sample at this point, add a drop of water to the slide just beside the coverslip.

7. When you are finished with the slide, wash it carefully using soap and water to remove all the cheek cells and iodine. Rinse the slide thoroughly.

What Did You See?

You saw small, irregularly shaped cheek cells. These cells do not look like **plant cells** (see pages 106–127) because they do not have cell walls. Instead, cheek cells, like all animal cells, have a thin covering called a cell **membrane**. The cell membrane contains the **cytoplasm**, or the inside part of the cell. Plant cells also have cell membranes, but they are inside the cell walls, which makes them hard to see.

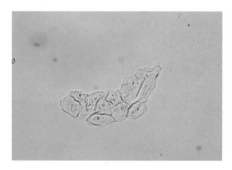
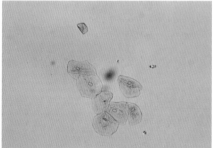

Cheek cells x400.

Cheek cells stained with iodine x400.

You also saw the **nucleus**, which is the small brown dot in the middle of the cell that was easier to see after you stained the cell. The nucleus contains the cell's DNA (see page 51). Your entire body is made up of cells. The cells in the lining of your cheek are constantly being replaced, so even though you removed some of them, new ones will grow in their place.

Cells

Cells make up your body and the bodies of every other living thing on the planet. Some creatures are made up of only a single cell (see sea life and pond life on pages 74–83), while others are made up of trillions of cells working together. All cells have cell membranes, and many of them have nuclei. There are other structures inside cells called **organelles**. These include the tiny cell parts in green plants called **chloroplasts** that use sunlight to help the cell produce sugar. **Mitochondria** are tiny organelles in cells that are used to turn sugar into the chemicals the cell uses for energy. The cells in crunchy vegetables such as celery and onion contain large liquid-filled **vacuoles** that are used for water storage. There are lots of other organelles found in cells, but these are the ones most likely to be seen using a home microscope.

Food Thief, or Dog vs. Cat

You left your lunch on a plate on the table and returned moments later to find your plate empty and one long hair on the table. Your dog and cat are hiding below your chair. Which pet do you think swiped your lunch? Can a microscope help you find the answer?

You Will Need

Fur from different animals, such as a cat, dog, rabbit, and hamster
Scissors
Slide and coverslip
Eyedropper
Water
Pencil and labels

What to Do

1. Brush your pet gently to remove a few hairs. Cut a piece of hair about ½-inch (1 cm) in length and make a wet mount of the hair.
2. Place the slide on the stage of the microscope and secure it with the stage clips.
3. Observe your slide using the low-power and high-power objectives. Record your observations.
4. Make more slides using the hair or fur from other pets. Make a slide of your own hair.
5. Observe these slides using the low-power and high-power objectives. Compare the different hair samples. Record your observations.

What Did You See?

The dog's fur was much thicker than the cat's fur. The cat's fur had very distinct scales compared with that of the dog. The medulla of the cat's fur looked like a stepladder and was very different from that of the dog's, which looked more like human hair.

While the color of a person's hair doesn't factor into his or her survival, animals have coverings that serve a purpose. Some sea mammals such as otters have thick fur that helps them float and protects them from the cold water. Polar bears have black skin, which absorbs heat, and whitish fur, which camouflages the bear. The hair of a sheep is thick, scaly, and oily, while the fur of a rabbit is smooth and very fine. Dog hair varies depending on the breed. Some dogs, such as poodles, have hair that is quite curly. Other breeds of dogs, such as Dalmatians, have short, straight hair. Cat hair is usually finer than dog hair but thicker than rabbit hair. Human hair varies in thickness but is usually thicker than cat or rabbit hair. The sizes of the three layers of hair are quite different in animals than they are in people. In animals, the medulla is usually thicker compared with the cortex than it is in humans. Some animals, such as sheep, have no medulla at all.

Cat hair x400.

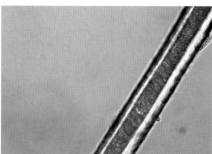

Dog hair x400.

Incriminating Evidence

Police use microscopes to help them solve crimes. As you've worked through the activities in this book, you have seen that evidence such as hair, fingerprints, and bits of thread can be collected and analyzed using a microscope. Special microscopes are used by law enforcement agencies to examine bullets. This equipment can compare two bullets at the same time to determine whether they were fired from the same weapon. While your microscope probably won't be able to show you the fine differences between bullets, you can perform a similar test using cellophane tape.

You Will Need

**Nail polish remover
with acetone**
**Clear, not frosted,
cellophane tape**
Cotton ball
Coins
Scissors
Coverslips
Slides
Microscope

What to Do

1. Use some nail polish remover and a 1-inch (2.5 cm) piece of cellophane tape to make an acetate peel of a coin, following the instructions on page 32.
2. Cut the piece of tape into two ½-inch (1.25 cm) sections so you can make two slides. Place each ½-inch piece of tape sticky side down on a separate coverslip. Place each coverslip on a slide with the tape in between. You now have 2 slides.
3. Repeat steps 1 and 2 with a different coin. You now have 4 slides. Label one slide in each pair with the type of surface (coin) used.
4. Place each slide on the stage of the microscope and secure it with the stage clips. Examine each slide under low- and high-power objectives. Try to determine which slides are the pairs.

What Did You See?

You could clearly see parts of the coin where the tape had been placed. The tape has adhesive, which is altered by the rough surface of the coin. The adhesive patterns were different for each of the surfaces you used.

The nail polish remover you used contains a chemical called **acetone**. Acetone softened the surface of the tape, which allowed it to form an impression in the shape of the coin. This technique can be used on any type of glass or metal surface, for example, the patterned handles of metal forks and spoons.

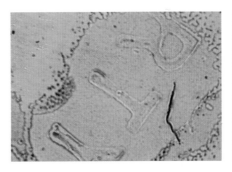

Cellophane peel of a penny x50.

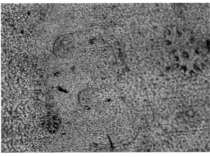

Cellophane peel of a penny x50.

Crystal Gazing

Sometimes liquids that have dried at a crime scene also provide clues. Here's how to create some beautiful crystalline structures and discover a technique that can be used with this type of evidence.

Is it really sugar?

You Will Need

Teaspoon

Water

Table salt

Slide

Solid samples such as sugar, borax, Epsom salts, alum (available at most drug stores)

Liquid samples such as from fresh rhubarb, lemon juice, orange juice, grapefruit juice

Pen

Paper

What to Do

1. Fill half a teaspoon with very warm water. Add a few grains of table salt to the teaspoon and allow the grains to dissolve.

2. Gently pour the mixture onto a clean slide. Make sure you label the slide so you'll know what you are looking at.

3. Move the slide to a windowsill and allow it to sit undisturbed until dry. This may take up to several days.

4. Make slides using the sugar, borax, Epsom salts, and alum following the same steps used for the table salt.

5. Squeeze some juice from the stem of a freshly cut rhubarb plant onto the center of a slide. Allow the liquid to evaporate. If you cannot find any rhubarb, try the juice from a fresh lemon, orange, or grapefruit instead.

6. Place each slide on the stage of the microscope and secure it with the stage clips. Observe your slides using the low-power and high-power objectives.

7. An interesting slide can also be made by drying out tears. Simply drop a tear onto a clean slide and allow it to dry. Compare the slide with the tear to that with the table salt. Do they look similar?

What Did You See?

Salt **crystals** formed on the slide when the water evaporated. Crystals are solids made from different types of salts. The tiny **particles** that make up the salts form a pattern. The patterns are repeated until billions of salt particles make larger crystals that have the same shape. Each type of salt has its own signature crystal shape. Table salt forms clear, colorless, cube-shaped crystals. The sugar sample is slower to form crystals. Epsom salts form hexagonal (6-sided) crystals. The different fruit samples are made up of several chemicals, so they have a mixture of crystal shapes and sizes.

Alum crystals x50.

Alum crystals x100.

Epsom crystals x10.

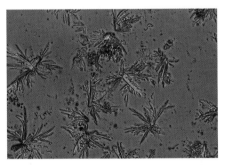

Rhubarb crystals x200.

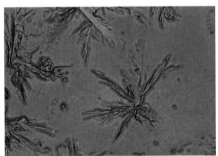

Rhubarb crystals x400.

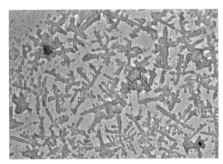

Tear crystals x200.

Salt crystals x50.

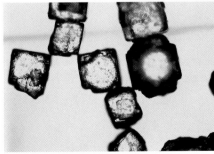

Salt crystals x100.

Sugar crystals x100.

April Fools!

A common April Fools' Day prank is to replace the sugar in the sugar bowl with salt. If you were a police scientist investigating these white crystals, you would not be able to taste them, as that could be dangerous. How could you tell what these substances were without putting them in your mouth?

Place a small amount of salt on a slide and view it under a microscope or even with a magnifying glass. Compare it with a known sample of sugar or artificial sugar. Which of the pictures at right does your sample most resemble?

Hawaiian salt under the dissecting microscope x6.

Salt under the dissecting microscope x12.

Sugar under the dissecting microscope x50.

Splenda under the dissecting microscope x12.

Those Can't Be Real!

Governments want to make sure that people don't **counterfeit**, or print their own money. To prevent this from happening, money is made from special material and contains security features. Let's see whether you can find some of these safeguards.

You Will Need

A new bill
A black light (optional)

Is it real?

What to Do

1. Place your bill under the stage clips on your microscope and study various sections of the bill under different magnifications. Can you find tiny words, letters, or pictures? Keep a record of the things you find.
2. If you can, try to place your bill under a black light. What can you see now?
3. Try steps 1 and 2 again, using money from other countries. Do these bills also contain hidden pictures?

What Did You See?

You may have found tiny words hidden on the bill, or you may have found that what look like wavy colored lines to the naked eye are not solid, but are actually words. If you had a black light, you might see the bills **fluoresce**, or glow, in different colors. These words, designs, and glow-in-the-dark threads are placed on currency to prevent people from photocopying or printing fake money. In addition, magnetic inks and special materials are used so that police and government officials can tell the difference between real and forged money.

Using UV light to examine a bill.

Did You Know?

Currency is not made using regular paper. To make them last longer and not disintegrate in the wash when you forget to take your allowance out of your pockets, bills are made from a mixture of cotton and linen fibers. This special material also gives the currency a unique texture, or feel, so experienced bank tellers can tell the difference between a real and a forged bill by touch.

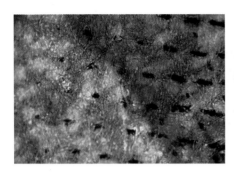

Light field view of $20 Canadian bill. You can also see the threads and materials used to make up the bill.

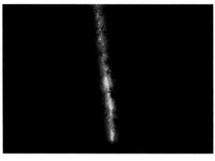

Same view of $20 Canadian bill under UV light.

Compare currencies from different countries. Which country has the most hidden words, symbols, or substances in its bills? Which the least? Research these countries and find out how many counterfeit bills are discovered in them each year. Is there a relationship between these two things?

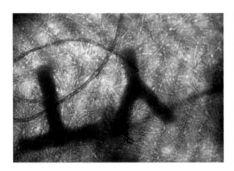

Light field view of $50 United States bill.

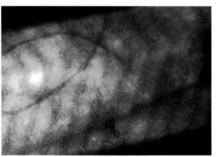

Same view of $50 United States bill under UV light.

Don't forget to study coins in addition to bills. Check out the humble American penny.

U.S. penny x12.

Part 3
Activities
Chapter 6
No Body but You

While you may think that you know your body, a microscope can help you discover some things you might—or mite—never have seen. You won't need to take blood or hurt yourself to find samples. Just about everything you need to examine is literally at your fingertips.

Dead Ends

Dead cells are covering your body. They flake off as dandruff and dry skin, or peel off when you have a sunburn. Here's a painless and simple way to get rid of some of these cells and study them under a microscope.

You Will Need

Clear cellophane tape (not the frosted type)
Slide

What to Do

1. Place a small strip of tape over a part of your body, such as your forehead, arm, or leg, and press the tape down firmly.
2. Hold one end of the tape and quickly pull it off your skin. It doesn't stick very much and won't hurt the way taking off a bandage might.
3. Place the tape on a slide with the sticky side facing up, and put a small drop of water on the center of the slide. Cover the slide with a coverslip.
4. View the tape under the microscope. What do you see?

What Did You See?

You saw dead skin cells, and depending on how clean your skin was, you might have also seen long, fat black blobs. These blobs are oil and dirt from the pores in your skin. Dead skin cells look different from your cheek cells because they are dried up; they have more jagged edges. In some cases you only saw part of a cell, as the cells broke apart when you removed the tape from your skin. You may also have seen very tiny hairs. These are the fine hairs that cover your skin, and they are much, much thinner than the hair on your head (see page 49–50).

Note: Tiny **mites** dine off the dead skin cells on your body. While it is theoretically possible to see them with a microscope, the authors were unable to locate any on their bodies or anyone else's.

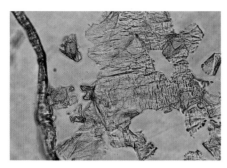

Skin cells from face x40.

Gunk from pores x40.

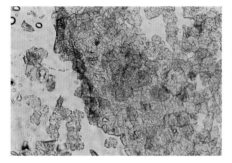

Skin cells from leg x40.

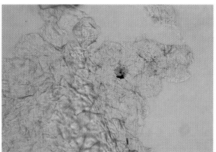

Skin cells from leg x400.

Toothpicks

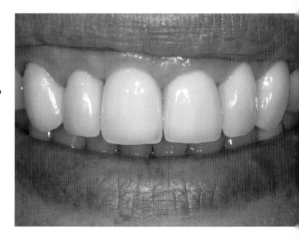

When you wake up in the morning, do your teeth ever feel slimy? During the night, **bacteria** grow in your mouth. If you never brushed or flossed your teeth, these bacteria would start to eat away at the coating on your teeth (the enamel), causing cavities. To give you an idea of what's happening in your mouth, here's an experiment that is guaranteed to encourage you to take extra care with your dental hygiene.

Note: This is a good experiment to do at home, but check with your teacher before doing it at school. For health reasons, some schools don't allow any experiments that might involve working with saliva.

You Will Need

Toothpick
Eyedropper
Slide and coverslip
Soap and water

Caution: **Use only your own mouth; do not use anyone else's.**

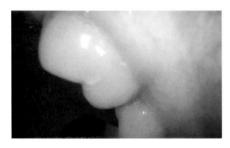

What to Do

1. Use a new, clean, wooden toothpick to gently scrape between your teeth or around your gums. You should not break the skin; just scrape the surface.
2. With an eyedropper, place two drops of water on a clean glass slide. Stir the toothpick back and forth in the water to transfer the sample. This will spread it out on the slide. Do not put the toothpick back into your mouth. Throw it away immediately.
3. Make a wet-mount slide of this sample, following the instructions on page 27.
4. Place the slide on the stage of the microscope and secure it with the stage clips.
5. Observe your slide using the low- and high-power objectives.
6. When you are finished with slide, wash it carefully using soap and water to remove the entire sample. Rinse the slide thoroughly.

What Did You See?

You may have seen small pieces of food, or bubbles from your saliva. There were probably some cells from the lining of your mouth, and also some **plaque**, which is the stuff that sticks to your teeth and contains bacteria, mucus, and dead cells. If you look really closely under high power, you may just be able to see something even more disgusting. There are tiny creatures growing in your mouth that look like small dots. These are bacteria. Bacteria are classified by their shapes. Rod-shaped bacteria are called **bacilli**. Small spherical bacteria clumped together like bunches of grapes are called **cocci**. Corkscrew-shaped bacteria are called **spirilla**.

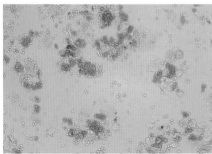

Bacteria from teeth x100.

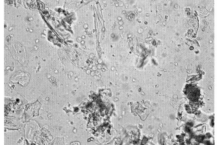

Bacteria from teeth x200.

Don't Sweat It

When you are hot or when you exercise really hard, **sweat** runs down your forehead and stings your eyes. What is in sweat, and what do you think it would look like under magnification?

You Will Need

Slide
Adult helper

What to Do

1. The next time you are really hot and sweaty, have an adult hold a slide under your arms or on your forehead. Find the spot where you have the most sweat and collect a sample on your slide.
2. Allow the sweat to dry on the slide; then place the slide on the stage of the microscope and secure it with the stage clips.
3. Observe your slide using the low- and high-power objectives.

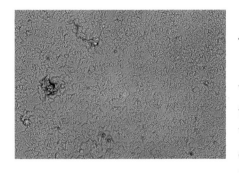

Sweat x50.

What Did You See?

You saw crystals that looked a bit like snowflakes. The crystals that formed are from your sweat. Sweat contains salts and water. When you let the water dry, it leaves behind the mixture of different salts, which form crystals. The chemicals that are found in sweat vary from person to person, and can even change with the foods you eat. Very pungent foods, such as onions or garlic, can scent your sweat if you eat them in large amounts. Phew! Why do you sweat? It's all about keeping cool. The water that sits on the surface of your skin cools you down. Some animals don't sweat very well, so instead they pant to cool down their insides, or they find other ways to keep their temperature down. Elephants and pigs roll around in mud, which they use as a natural air conditioner: The water in the mud evaporates because of the animal's body heat and so cools the animal's body, leaving a "dirt sunblock" behind.

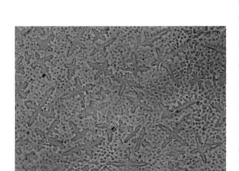

Sweat x400.

Reflective Nails

Cosmetic companies like to advertise that their product is the shiniest on the market. But just what makes a polish shine and glimmer in the sun? Let's see what we can find under the microscope.

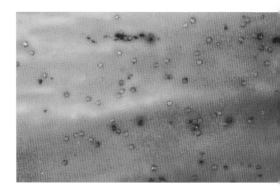

Red shiny nail polish under the dissecting microscope x6.

You Will Need

Different kinds of shiny nail polish
Slides

What to Do

1   Lightly coat a small section of a slide with nail polish. Try different colors and kinds. Allow the nail polish to dry completely.
2. Place the slide on the stage of the microscope and secure it with the stage clips.
3. Observe the slide using the low- and high-power objectives.

What Did You See?

As you can see here, there are tiny, metallic-looking bits in the polish. These bits may be made from various materials, such as the mineral **mica**, which act as miniature mirrors to reflect the light that hits the coated nail. This is why certain polishes shine in the light. Other types of makeup, such as lipstick, contain a sparkly material called **pearlescence** that is made from fish scales.

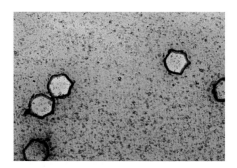

The same nail polish x50 under the light microscope.

Part 3
Activities
Chapter 7
Creature Features

We don't recommend killing any creature to study it under a microscope, but sometimes you can find a convenient bug that is already dead. Small creatures—especially insects—do not live very long and expire in handy locations, such as windowsills.

Convenient Bug

Once you are certain that a bug is dead, use a pair of tweezers to gently place the bug in a small container to transport the bug to the microscope. Put the bug on a slide and examine its features under the microscope. Here's a great opportunity to see the **facets** on a bug's eye, the **sensory hairs** on its body, and even the pollen on the legs of a bee.

Fly x6.

Fly eye x50.

Flies are very good at evading swatters. This is because they have very large, compound eyes. As you can see in the picture, flies' eyes have many shiny little dots. Each of these dots, called **ommatidia**, is like a tiny eye. Having these "extra" eyes helps the fly see the swatter's approach.

About 100 years ago, if something was really cool, a child might say it was the "bee's knees." Well, bees don't have knees, but you may find pollen from various flowers dusting the legs of the bee. Bees have special baskets on their legs where they store the pollen, which they use as a source of protein to make honey.

Bee leg pollen x12.

Honeycomb x25.

Viewing insects under a microscope is a great way to compare a bee's body with that of a wasp. You can see that the wasp's body is more slender than a bee's. A bee's body is covered with "hair" that the pollen can rub off on.

Wasp top side x6.

Wasp side x6.

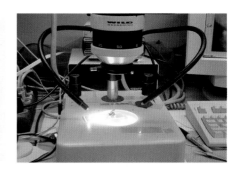

Authors' dissecting microscope with wasp.

Compare the wings of the wasp and bee to those of the fly. Flies are unusual because they have only one pair of wings, while most other flying insects have two pairs. On flies, where the second pair of wings would normally be, is instead a pair of knoblike structures called halteres. The halteres move up and down to act like tiny rudders.

Bee wing x12.

Wasp wing x25.

Warning: Do not touch a stinging insect with your hands. Use a pair of tweezers to handle the bug. Note: If an adult has used a commercial foam spray to coat a wasp nest, do not knock this nest down to study it. The wasp larvae may not, in fact, be dead.

Bee stinger x12.

Wasp stinger x12.

Spit or Spittle Bug

Scientists have always thought that fleas were the best jumpers in the insect world, but it turns out that spit bugs are the champion jumpers. What makes them particularly interesting is their foamy spit. Spit normally comes from your mouth, but in the case of the spit bug it comes from the other end. The spit bug uses this foam for protection, to hide from creatures that eat it. It also keeps the bug moist and cool in summer.

Spit bug's foam protection.

Spit bug x12.

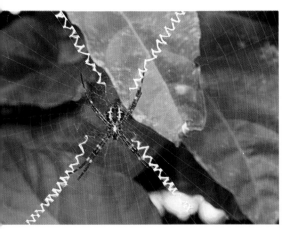
Orb web with zigzags.

Charlotte's Parlor

See whether you can find a spider's web early in the morning when the web is glistening with dew. You can see the water hanging in little droplets along the strands of the web. A spider's web makes a wonderful microscope sample, but you have to wait until it's dry so it will stick to the slide! Using a microscope, you can begin to understand why insects, once trapped, cannot escape from the sticky web.

You Will Need

Slide
Clear nail polish
Dry, empty garden spider's web
Stick
Coverslip

What to Do

1. Cover the center of a slide with a thin layer of colorless nail polish. Allow the nail polish to set for about 1 minute.
2. Quickly place the slide on the center part of the web and pull the web toward you. Use a stick to knock away the outer edge of the web, so that it does not stick to you or the slide.
3. Immediately cover the slide with the coverslip and press down gently.
4. Place the slide on the stage of the microscope and secure it with the stage clips.
5. Examine your slide under both the low-power and high-power objectives.

What Did You See?

The type of spider web you collected is called an **orb web**, formed by the common garden spider. It looks like it is made of spokes moving outward like the spokes of a wheel. The spider uses the sticky fibers of this web to catch small insects, which it eats. The strands of silk from the web have 2 parts: a long, elastic fiber and drops of gooey stuff. When the spider spins a web, it releases the web material from small pores called spinnerets located between its back legs. The web material is made by silk glands inside the spider. Different kinds of spider webs are formed by other kinds of spiders.

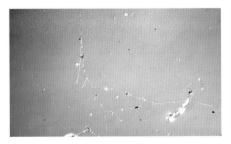

Spider web x50.

Spider web x100.

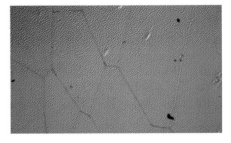

Spider web x200.

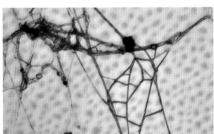

Spider web x630.

Did You Know?

The type of spider that built the web shown at far left is called an argiope spider. The **argiope spider** builds an orb web that often has a heavy zigzag part in the middle called a **stabilimenta**. Scientists aren't sure why the spiders use the stabilimenta. It may be to make the web stronger or tighter, for protection from birds, or to attract insects.

Birds of a Feather

Many tropical birds have brightly colored feathers. These feathers may be one color on top and another on the bottom. Peacocks have long colorful feathers; ostriches and emus have big fluffy feathers. Geese and ducks have thick, stiff feathers, while chicks and other baby birds have soft, downy feathers. By examining some of these feathers under a microscope, you can begin to see the differences in the types of feathers.

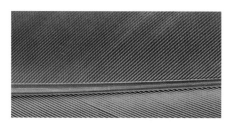

Macaw feather.

Back of same macaw feather.

You Will Need

Different kinds of feathers
Scissors
Eyedropper
Glycerine
Slides
Tweezers
Coverslips
Tissue or paper towel

What to Do

1. Gather several different kinds of feathers. A good source of feathers might be your local zoo or bird sanctuary. Ask the staff whether they can give you some of the feathers from the birds' cage or pen. Look around a park or even your yard for bird feathers. If you own a bird, gather feathers from the bottom of the cage. Some craft shops also sell individual feathers.
2. Use scissors to cut a small section, on either side of the shaft, from the feather. You may wish to cut several sections from different parts of the feather.
3. Use the eyedropper to place 2 drops of glycerine on the center of the slide.
4. Place the feather sample on the glycerine using the tweezers. Hold the coverslip upright so that one edge of the slip touches the edge of the drops of glycerine. Gently lower the coverslip over the glycerine and sample, trying not to trap any air bubbles. Blot up excess glycerine with a tissue or paper towel.
5. Record in your journal the type of feather and section location.
6. Place the slide on the stage of the microscope and secure it with the stage clips.
7. Examine your slide under both the low-power and high-power objectives.
8. Make several samples using different kinds of feathers.

What Did You See?

You saw dark lines that crossed the microscope slide. These lines are the parts of the feather. The parts of the feather are different depending on the kind of feather you are looking at.

There are three main types of feathers: contour feathers, down feathers, and filoplumes. **Contour** feathers are the large feathers that cover the bird's body. They have a central **shaft** and **vanes**, or branches, which grow out from the feather's center shaft. Little hooks, or **barbules**, hold the tiny strands of the feather to each other. **Down** feathers are small, soft feathers underneath the contour feathers. They are simpler, and don't have barbules. Down feathers keep the birds warm. **Filoplumes**, or hairlike feathers, are thin feathers with a single, hairlike shaft. The colorful feathers of peacocks are filoplumes.

Feather x50.

Feather x100.

Feather x50.

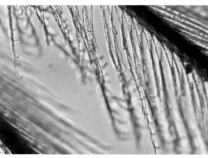

Feather x200.

Did You Know?

Feathers on most female birds are drab, while the feathers on male birds are generally colorful. The male birds use this beautiful plumage to attract the attention of the opposite sex. The feathers on females are dull so they blend into the background while the females sit on their eggs. The feathers of some tropical birds such as the macaw are two different colors: when you see them from below, the blue in their feathers blends in with the color of the sky; from above, other colors in their feathers look like the ground.

Front of macaw feather under the dissecting microscope x50.

Back of same macaw feather under the dissecting microscope x50.

Chapter 8

Don't Drink the Water

If a day spent around water is your idea of a good time, you will love this next section. It doesn't matter whether you live near a lake, river, marsh, stream, or ocean; any kind of natural water is a great place to find samples. And if you don't like the water, don't worry—even a pet store or a seafood store can provide you with samples.

Sounds Fishy to Me

When we think of what a fish looks like, we generally imagine a scaly creature that lives in the water. Just as birds' feathers give them unique characteristics, fishes' scales have their own patterns by which they can be identified. Not only will this experiment show you some of the differences between fish scales, but you also will be able to tell the age of a fish.

Note: For this activity you need a really small, single fish scale, not a large piece of fish skin. You may be able to visit a fish market and ask for a small sample of scales. These stores are often more than happy to give you a sample, and you will not have harmed any creature to obtain it. Keep the scales damp in a plastic bag until you can study them at home.

Fish scales under the dissecting microscope x12.

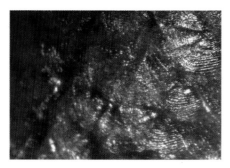

Fish scales under the dissecting microscope x25.

What You Need

Small scales from different kinds of fish (e.g., goldfish, trout)
Paper towel
Water
Small container
Eyedropper
Slides
Tweezers
Coverslip
Pen
Paper

What to Do

1. Ask for samples of different fish scales at the grocery store or at a specialty store that sells fresh seafood. Try to get scales that are pulled from the fish. When a salesperson places a fresh fish on a piece of butcher's paper and lifts the fish off, usually a perfect sample of scales is left on the paper.
2. Wrap each type of fish scale in wet paper toweling, and label each package so that you can tell what kind of fish it came from. Place the wet toweling in a container to take home.
3. Unwrap each package of fish scales just before you wish to examine it. If your fish scales are really slimy, wipe off some of the moisture on a paper towel.
4. Make a wet mount of each individual fish scale following the instructions on page 27.
5. Place the slide on the stage of the microscope and secure it with the stage clips.
6. Examine your slide under the low-power objective.
7. Make a record of the type of fish, the number of rings on the scale, the color of the scale, and the size of the scale.

What Did You See?

Scales are unique to each type of fish. If you look at a fish, you will notice that the scales overlap or attach to a fish in the same manner as the shingles do to a roof. If you were constructing a fish, you would put the first layer of scales on at the tail, and place subsequent rows one atop the previous one, ending up with the last row at the fish's head.

Some fish, such as tuna, have interlocking scales. Over the years, the structure of this fish has changed so that the scales now mesh together. Fish such as salmon have large, shiny scales. Sharks, on the other hand, don't have scales at all. They have rough, sandpaper-like skin. Their skin has tiny projections called **denticles**, which make their skin feel as if it were covered with tiny teeth.

Scientists are able to tell the type or species of fish by examining the scales. Each type of fish has a special pattern of scales. You can tell something about the age of the fish by counting the rings on the scales. The older the fish is, the more rings there are on the scales.

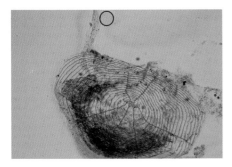

Goldfish scales x50.

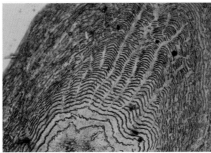

Halibut scales x50.

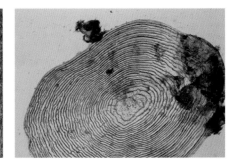

Trout scales x50.

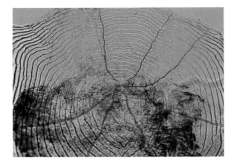

Goldfish scales x100.

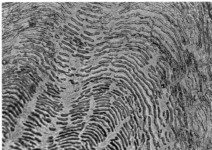

Halibut scales x100.

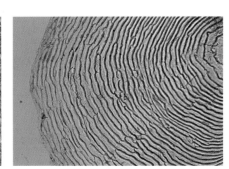

Trout scales x100.

Sharkskin Suits

Swimwear manufacturers have studied sharkskin and incorporated sharkskin-like material into swim-suit designs. The fabric used for racing suits worn by competitive swimmers has small bumps that act like the denticles, smoothing out the flow around the swimmer and reducing drag.

Sharkskin material for clothing.
Courtesy Dr. Elaine Humphrey.

Water, Water Everywhere

The oceans, lakes, ponds, and ditches of the world are filled with tiny living things. There are more small things living in a single drop of water than you may realize. Don't expect to find them swimming around in your drinking water, though. Most people drink water that has been purified and therefore should not contain these small creatures. (If you do find them in your drinking water, tell your parents and the appropriate authorities!)

Here is a simple way to collect samples, and two different techniques to view them.

Note: Pond water should not be stored near food. Glassware and hands that have handled pond water should be washed thoroughly with soap and water. Clean up any spills of pond water with disinfectant. Do not eat or touch your eyes, nose, or mouth when handling pond water.

You Will Need

Large storage jar and lid
Thin piece of cloth, large enough to cover the top of the jar
Elastic band
Pond, freshwater lake, or river water
Uncooked rice
Adult helper

What to Do

1. Take your large storage jar to the pond, lake, or river to collect your sample. Be sure to take an adult helper. You might want to use a ladle or other utensil to scoop the water into the container.
2. Put some of the water into your jar. Add some of the leaves of plants growing at the edge of the water.
3. Scoop some of the dirt from the bottom of the pond, lake, or river and add it to the jar.
4. Cover the jar with the lid and secure it with the elastic band. It is important to wash your hands with soap and water after handling pond water.
5. When you get home, follow the instructions on page 33 for making a rice infusion.
6. Place the slide on the stage of the microscope and secure it with the stage clips.
7. Observe your slide under the low- and high-power objectives.

What Did You See?

You should have seen tiny little creatures in the water. They may be rather strange looking, and they may even resemble something from an old science fiction movie! Some of the creatures are plants like the **algae** (**spirogyra**) samples you see in the micrographs shown here, some are single-celled organisms, and others are simple animals like the worm (**oligochete**) and the water flea (**daphnia**) shown in the micrographs. These are a few of the common freshwater creatures you may see, but there are many others.

Protozoa

Scientists have named about 10,000 different types of 1-celled **organisms**, known collectively as **protozoa**. These creatures live in water all over the world. Have you ever wondered how they get into the ponds and puddles in the first place? They can live in dry conditions, on plants or in the soil, for long periods of time. They do this by forming a protective covering known as a **cyst**. When they get wet, they break out of their cysts and become active once again.

Pond worm x15.

Strands of cotton are used to trap a creature from a drop of water x100.

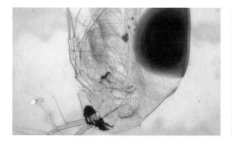

Water flea x50.

Water flea x100.

Microscopists sometimes use special slides called "well slides." These slides have a small bowl-shaped well in the middle. This well is useful when you are looking at living specimens contained in liquids such as pond water. If you have a well slide, you can use it to look at pond creatures. If not, make one following the instructions on page 29.

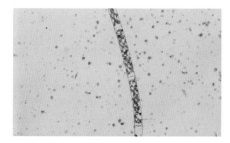

Algae x100.

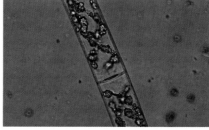

Algae x200.

See Life

If you live near the ocean, you can find some of the most amazing creatures there. A thimbleful of water can be teeming with life.

You Will Need

Sand shovel

A small bucket or plastic
  sealable bags

Adult helper

Slides

Cotton balls

Eyedropper

Rice

What to Do

1. At low tide, find a shallow tidal pool and use your shovel to scoop a small amount of water, seaweed, and sand into a bucket or plastic bag. Do not gather too much sand. The water should look slightly murky.
2. When you get home, follow the instructions on page 33 for making a rice infusion.
3. Observe your slide under the low- and high-power objectives.
4. Make a well slide following the instructions on page 29, and use an eyedropper to add a few drops of the collected seawater to the slide.
5. Place the slide on the stage of the microscope and secure it with the stage clips.
6. Observe your well slide under low power. If you want to increase the magnification, be very careful when focusing your microscope; the thicker well slide may be able to touch your objective lens. Be careful when using water with salts dissolved in it. The salts can be corrosive to both your objective lenses and any metal parts of your microscope. If salt water spills onto your microscope, carefully wipe it up and make sure no salts remain.

What Did You See?

There are different kinds of creatures in the ocean water than there are in pond or freshwater. Some of these creatures are babies, like the **nauplius** shown below, which will grow up to be a **barnacle**. Baby barnacles are free swimming, but the adults attach themselves to surfaces such as rocks, boats, or piers and form a protective shell. Some barnacles are even found on the skin of whales. The adult **copepod** in the photo is carnivorous (it eats other creatures). Other types of these creatures eat only algae. You can also find **diatoms** (see page 83) floating in the water. We also found an **amphipod** in our sample, but your sample could contain many different types of marine life, depending on where you live and the time of the year you collect your sample.

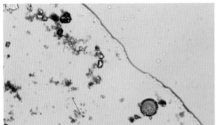

Seawater x200.

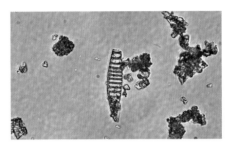

Diatoms x400.

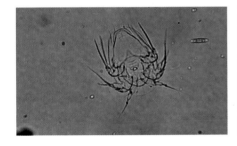

Barnacle nauplius x400.

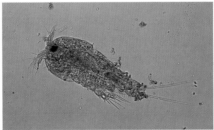

Copepod x200.

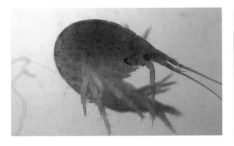

Amphipod x12.

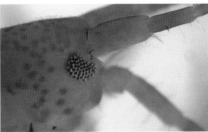

Amphipod x25.

Did You Know?

Diatoms use their shells as homes or for protection, but why do people use them? Diatomaceous earth is used as a filtering material for swimming pools and as an abrasive or polishing material in metal polish. It even has been used as a polishing agent in toothpaste. It can also be used as an insecticide and as an absorbent in kitty litter.

Smile! Diatoms are very photogenic. A hundred years ago, before wide-screen LCD TVs existed, an evening's entertainment might have consisted of viewing slides of beautifully arranged diatoms. Individual diatoms were painstakingly placed in kaleido-scope patterns, permanently mounted, and then viewed with a microscope. Some museums have samples of these antique slides.

See page 83 for the diatom activity.

Cotton the Act

Sometimes ocean or pond creatures are difficult to see because they zip about through the water so quickly. You can slow them down by adding chemicals to the water, but this may kill them. Here is a gentler method of slowing them down.

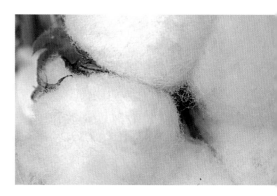

You Will Need

Cotton ball
Slide
Eyedropper
Pond or ocean water
Coverslip

Cotton strands trap a creature x200.

What to Do

1. Follow the procedure for "Trapping Living Things" (page 34) by pulling several strands from the cotton ball and place them in the center of the slide; use an eyedropper to place a drop or two of pond or ocean water on top of the cotton strands; and gently place the coverslip on top of the water and cotton-strand sample. Do not press down.
2. Place the slide on the stage of the microscope and secure it with the stage clips.
3. Look at your slide using the low-power objective. You may have to reduce the amount of light going through the diaphragm to see the creatures more easily.
4. When you have found some of the creatures, place them in the center of your field of view and look at them with the high-power objective.

What Did You See?

The pond animals were slowed down by the cotton strands. They could not move as fast because the strands of cotton were in their way. The cotton strands also held the coverslip up higher, giving the organisms room to move.

Creature trapped in cotton strands x400.

Glass Houses

Diatoms

What would it be like to live in a glass house? Other than the fact you wouldn't want stones thrown at it, there is a creature whose home is made from **silica**, the material used to make glass. You can find some of these cool creatures if you know where to look.

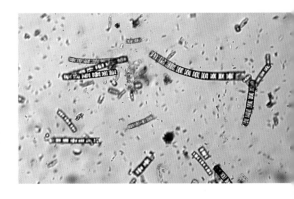

Diatoms x100.

You Will Need

Tweezers
Diatomaceous earth (found in garden and hardware stores)
Slides
Coverslips

What to Do

1. Use your tweezers to take a small sample of diatomaceous earth from the container.
2. Place sample on a slide and make a wet mount, following the instructions on page 27.
3. Place the slide on the stage of the microscope and secure it with the stage clips.
4. View the slide under the low- and high-power objectives. What kinds of diatoms did you find?

What Did You See?

You could see different forms of **diatom** shells. Diatoms are a type of single-celled algae that have cell walls containing silica. They make up most of the **phytoplankton**, the layer of living matter that floats near the surface of the ocean and in lakes. **Diatomaceous** earth can contain whole diatom shells, but usually you will find only parts of the shells. There are two main types of diatoms: the **pennates**, which are shaped like pens; and the **centric**, which are cylinder shaped.

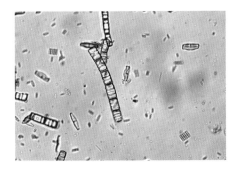

Diatoms x200.

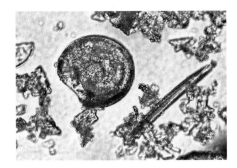

Diatoms x400.

Part 3
Activities
Chapter 9
Food for Thought

What do you get when you have eggs, onions, olives, and mushrooms? No, not the makings of a great omelet, but rather the beginnings of the materials you'll need for the next section. Things in your fridge provide for some fascinating viewing under the microscope. Just remember not to snack on your experiments!

Scrambled or Fried?

**A box without hinges, key, or lid,
Yet golden treasure inside is hid.
—J.R.R. Tolkien**

What is the answer to this riddle? That's right. This is an egg. An egg is one giant cell. The holes you see in the photographs are some of the thousands of tiny pores on the surface of the egg. The pores allow the egg to take in oxygen and let out **carbon dioxide** and water. Let's take a closer look at your breakfast.

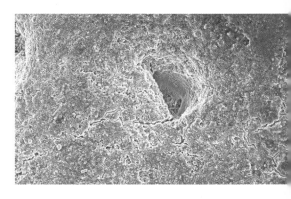

Scanning electron microscope image of pore in surface of eggshell. Courtesy Dr. Elaine Humphrey.

Whole eggshell showing pores in normal light.

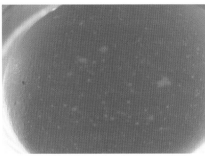

Light shining through eggshell.

You Will Need

Fresh, raw egg
Soap and water
Paper towel
Bowl
Tweezers
Slide
Antibacterial soap and water

What to Do

1. Wash the outside of the eggshell with soap and water and dry it with a paper towel.
2. Crack open the egg and place the egg in a bowl. (You can give the egg to an adult to put away or use for cooking.)
3. Use your tweezers to pull a small section of egg membrane from the inner part of the shell. Place this membrane on a slide and make a wet mount, following the instructions on page 27.
4. View the slide under different magnifications.

Warning: It is important to wash your hands and all surfaces the egg has touched with antibacterial soap. Throw away the egg, slides, and eggshell after you have finished your activity.

Did You Know?

The shell of an egg is made from crystals of **calcite**, a chemical that contains **calcium**. Many people drink milk because of the calcium, which builds strong bones, but chickens don't drink milk, so where do they get the nutrients they need to make eggshells? Good question. Chicken are fed a special meal or grain rich in calcium. They store this calcium in their bones, and their bodies use this calcium when they lay eggs. It has been observed that younger chickens lay thicker eggs than older hens.

It takes a lot of effort for a chicken to make an egg. The shell itself takes 15 to 16 hours to form in the hen, and the average hen lays an egg every couple of days. In fact the hen that holds the record for egg-laying produced only 361 eggs in a year.

Eggs from different breeds of chickens are different sizes. Check the sides of egg containers the next time you are in the grocery store. Can you find these eggs?

Egg Sizes
Peewee—Less than 1.5 ounces (42 grams)
Small—1.5 oz (42 g) to 1.69 oz (48 g)
Medium—1.7 oz (49 g) to 1.99 oz (55 g)
Large—2 oz (56 g) to 2.24 oz (63 g)
Extra large—2.25 oz (64 g) to 2.44 oz (69 g)
Jumbo—More than 2.44 oz (69 g)

Eggshell halves, showing thin inner membrane.

What Did You See?

You saw the thin **membrane** that sits between the shell and the egg. This membrane acts as a filter that keeps bacteria out and helps to keep the egg from spoiling. The egg also takes in oxygen from the air. The pores in the membrane can take in more than just oxygen; they can also take in odors. You might want to store eggs away from smelly things, like blue cheese or chopped onions, in the fridge.

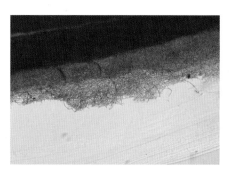

Edge of tissue membrane from egg x50.

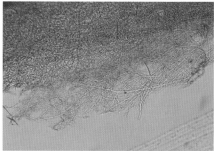

Edge of tissue membrane from egg x100.

Onion Rings

As strange as this may sound to you, the onion in your fridge or cupboard is a living thing. If you examine a slice of onion under a microscope, you will see the specialized plant cells contained in the see-through lining. Don't worry about crying when you peel the onion to prepare the sample for this activity; you can use your tears as part of the experiment on page 56!

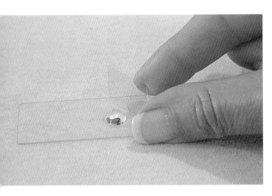

Making a wet mount of the onion skin sample. Photo courtesy El'ad Tzadok.

You Will Need

Raw cooking onion
Knife (to be handled by an
  adult only) ▰
Tweezers
Eyedropper
Water
Slide
Coverslip
Tissue or paper towel
Tincture of iodine (available in
  most drugstores)

What to Do

1. Have an adult slice the raw onion and cut one of the onion rings into ½-inch (1.25-cm) sections.
2. Remove the thin skin from the outer, convex side of the section by pulling it gently with tweezers. You could also try bending a longer piece of the onion ring and gently pulling the skin as it peels from the section.
3. Make a wet mount of the onion skin, following the instructions on page 27, and flattening the onion skin in the drop of water.
4. Examine your slide under both the low-power and high-power objectives.

Big, Bigger, Biggest

There is a limit to how many times your microscope can magnify specimens. If you really wanted to get up close and personal with a sample, you would need a **scanning electron microscope** (SEM). The SEM moves a beam of focused electrons across the object, and then the electrons produced and scattered by the object are collected to form a three-dimensional image. In the images below, you can find the scale bar that is labeled 20 μm to get a sense of just how close the SEM got; one micrometer (μm), also called micron, is one-millionth of a meter, one–one thousandth of a millimeter, or approximately 1/25,000 of an inch. Don't bother looking for one of these microscopes in your local store; universities and research facilities are the only places where you can find them.

Scanning electron microscope image of the surface of eggshell. Courtesy Dr. Elaine Humphrey.

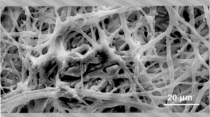

Scanning electron microscope image of the structure of eggshell. Courtesy Dr. Elaine Humphrey.

5. Remove your slide from the microscope and place it on a piece of tissue or paper towel.
6. Stain the sample with tincture of iodine by pulling the stain, following the directions on page 30.
7. Place the slide on the stage of the microscope and secure it with the stage clips.
8. Examine your slide under both the low-power and high-power objectives. Compare these images with those you saw when you looked at the onion skin without the iodine stain.

What Did You See?

When you looked at the onion skin under the microscope, you saw rows of long 6-sided boxes. The boxes are the cells of the onion skin. You may have seen a little blob that looked like a bubble inside some of the cells. This is called the **cell nucleus**. Staining the cells with the tincture of iodine makes it easier to see the cells and their parts. The iodine makes most parts of the cell yellow and the nucleus yellowish brown. The parts of the onion skin that you can probably see with your microscope are the **cell wall**, which is the nonliving support for the cell; the nucleus, which directs the cell's activities; and the cytoplasm, which is the fluid inside the cell. You may also see vacuoles, which store waste materials and water in the cell. Onion skin cells are used by the onion for protection, especially from drying out and from insects.

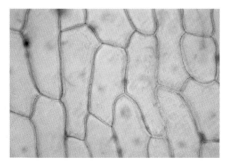

Onion skin x200.

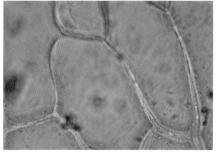

Onion skin x400.

Onion Tears

Why do you cry when you're cutting onions? Onions contain **acids** that irritate your eyes. Acids are typically water-soluble and sour compounds that in solution are capable of reacting with a base to form a salt. The tear glands in your eyes produce tears to flush out these irritating chemicals.

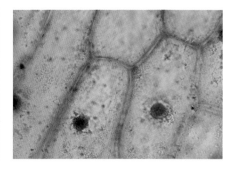

Onion skin x100, stained with iodine.

Onion skin x400, stained with iodine.

Getting to the Root of Things

Throughout this book you will have an opportunity to study various parts of plants. In the pollen section (page 114), you can view the top part of a plant. The stem is examined on pages (108), and at the bottom of the plant you'll find the root.

The root is one of the most important parts of the plant. Without the root, the plant could not take in the water or nutrients it needs to live. The root anchors the plant to the soil so that it does not blow away. Here's a simple way to grow some roots.

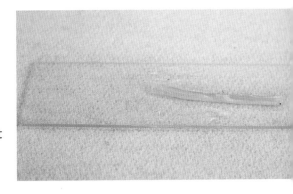

A squash slide made of onion root.
Photo courtesy El'ad Tzadok.

You Will Need

A fresh green onion
Water
Knife (to be handled by an adult only) ▰
Tweezers
Carrot
Homemade microtome (see page 36)
Eyedropper
Water
Slides
Coverslips

Note: Root hairs are very fragile and damage easily. You must be careful not to squash them or hold them too tightly, as it will then be difficult to prepare a good slide.

What to Do

1. Use a fresh green onion with long white roots, or you can use the roots of a white onion if they are white and look fresh.
2. Have an adult cut 2 roots from the onion with a kitchen knife.
3. The homemade microtome can be used to slice a lengthwise section of onion root, but that is very tricky. Better to have an adult prepare a piece of root by slicing a ½-inch (1.25-cm) section of root lengthwise from the tip of the root to the end. Use the tweezers to carefully transfer the root sample to the slide. Make a wet mount of this section following the instructions on page 27.
4. Examine your slide under both the low-power and high-power objectives. Make note of what this section looks like.
5. Use the second piece of onion root to prepare a squash slide following the instructions on page 31.
6. Place the slide on the stage of the microscope and secure it with the stage clips.
7. Examine your slide under both the low-power and high-power objectives

What Did You See?

The outer layer, or **epidermis**, of the root is made up of small cells. Inside these cells are larger, light-colored cortex cells, which make up the bulk of the root. There are bundles of darker cells, called **xylem** and **phloem** cells, through which the roots transport water and nutrients to the plant. In the long section of the root, these cells look like oblong boxes. These cells act like tubes to move the water and nutrients up into the stems and the leaves of the plant.

In the squash sample, you saw the cells that make up the root. It is much easier to squash the root than to slice it, so if you can't make a thin enough sliced sample, don't despair—squash!

Onion root tip section x100.

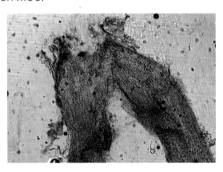

Onion root tip squash sample x50.

Onion root tip squash sample x100.

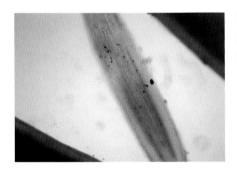

Onion root tip squash sample x200.

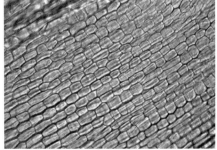

Onion root tip squash sample x400.

Nothing Rhymes with Purple

Have you ever wondered why purple onions are a different color than regular cooking onions? When mixed with other ingredients, they sometimes even change color. This is because purple onions contain a colored chemical, or **pigment**, called **anthocyanin**. Anthocyanin acts as an **indicator**. Indicators are chemicals that change color if they are mixed with acids or bases. Let's look at the colors the onion can become.

You Will Need

Raw purple onion
Knife (to be handled by an
  adult only)
Tweezers
Eyedropper
Water
Slide
Coverslip
Tissue or paper towel
Vinegar, baking soda, and salt
Measuring cup and spoon
Microscope

A sample of purple onion skin.

What to Do

1. Have an adult slice the raw purple onion and cut one of the onion rings into ½-inch (1.25-cm) sections.

2. Remove the thin skin from the outer, convex side of the onion section by pulling it gently with tweezers. Cut the skin into 3 pieces each about ½-inch (1.25 cm) square.

3. Make three wet mounts of the onion skin following the instructions on page 27 and flattening each piece of the onion skin in a drop of water.

4. Place the slide on the stage of the microscope and secure it with the stage clips.

5. Examine your first slide under the microscope, using both the low-power and high-power objectives.

6. Place a few drops of vinegar on one side of the coverslip and hold a corner of the paper towel near the other side of the coverslip. The vinegar will move underneath the coverslip. Watch the effect of the vinegar on the onion skin.

7. Place the slide on the stage of the microscope and secure it with the stage clips.

8. Examine your second slide under the microscope, using both the low-power and high-power objectives.

9. Dissolve 1 tablespoon (15 ml) of baking soda in ? cup (125 ml) of warm water. Stir to dissolve. This is your baking soda solution.

10. Place a few drops of the baking soda solution on one side of the coverslip and hold a corner of the paper towel near the other side of the coverslip. The baking soda solution will move underneath the coverslip. Watch the effect of this solution on the onion skin.

11. Dissolve 1 tablespoon (15 ml) of salt in ½-cup (125 ml) of warm water. Stir to dissolve. This is your salt solution.

12. Place a few drops of the salt solution on one side of the coverslip and hold a corner of the paper towel near the other side of the coverslip. The salt solution will move underneath. Watch the effect of this solution on the onion skin.

What Did You See?

You saw the long, box-shaped onion skin cells contained in the nonliving cell walls. Inside the cell walls is a thin cell membrane. The cell membrane contains the cytoplasm, or fluid, inside the cell. The pigment, anthocyanin, is in the cytoplasm. When you looked at the onion cells in each of the slides at the beginning of the experiment, you saw that they were purple.

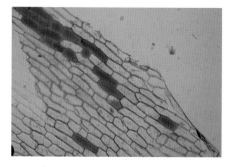

Purple onion skin x50.

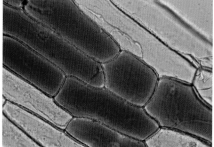

Purple onion skin x200.

When the vinegar was added, the cells became more **acidic**. As they became more acidic, they turned a lighter, redder color. When the baking soda solution was added, the cells became less acidic, or more **basic**. As they became less acidic, they turned a bluer purple and sometimes they became completely blue or green.

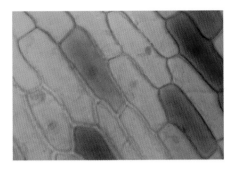

Purple onion skin x200, with vinegar added.

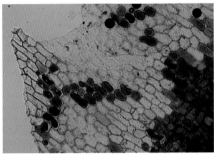

Purple onion skin x50, with baking soda added.

The salt did something different to the onion cells. Adding salt water made the water inside the cells move out in a process called osmosis. There was less cytoplasm than before and the insides of the cells looked shriveled.

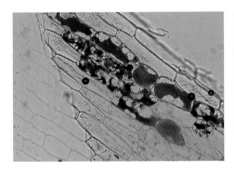

Purple onion skin x100, with salt added.

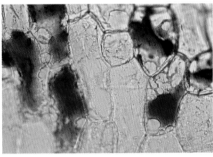

Purple onion skin x200, after salt added.

Science Fair

Here is another experiment that you could develop into a Science Fair project. Onion skin and other plant materials containing pigments that act as indicators can be used to test materials for acidity. A good substitute for purple onion is purple cabbage. Have an adult chop up 2 cups (500 ml) of cabbage and place it in a bowl. Then ask the adult to pour 4 cups (1 L) of very hot water over the chopped-up cabbage. Strain the cabbage and use the colored water to test materials. Acids will be red and bases will be blue or green. You can even soak a clean coffee filter in this mixture, allow it to dry, and cut it into strips to use as acidity indicator test strips similar to litmus paper, which is made from complex plant-like **lichens** (see "Did You Know?" on page 95).

Webs and Gills

Ducks have webbed feet and fish have gills, but what does this have to do with mushrooms? It turns out that mushrooms also have webs and gills, but not the same kind as ducks and fish. The webs on mushrooms are called the **mycelium**, and they are found under the ground. Mushrooms grow at the outside edge of a circular mat of weblike mycelium. The mat grows from the location where the spore is first buried under the ground and extends outward in all directions. The mushrooms usually form on the outer edge of the web, sometimes in a circle. These circles were called "fairy rings" in European folktales because they often appeared overnight. The most common types of mushrooms have gills. The gills of the mushroom are the frilly pieces found just under the cap. These gills have little knobs on them, which contain the **spores** of the mushroom. Spores are used to grow new mushrooms. Mushrooms belong to a group called the **fungi**. Other members of this group include **molds** and **yeasts**.

Warning: Do not taste or eat any mushrooms that you have gathered from the garden or forest; they may be poisonous. Wash your hands and equipment with soap and water after this experiment and be sure to throw away any unknown mushrooms when you are done so they aren't mistaken for food.

Preparing a slide with the mushroom cap gill-side down.

This Amanita is one of many in a group that includes some deadly poisonous forms that should be avoided and not handled.

You Will Need

Several different kinds of fresh mushrooms

Slides

Labels

Pencil

What to Do

1. Pull out the stem of a mushroom and place the mushroom gill side down on a slide. Leave this sample someplace warm overnight.
2. The next day, take the mushroom off the slide. You should see brown lines on the slide.
3. Place the slide on the stage of the microscope and secure it with the stage clips.
4. Observe your slide using the low-power and high-power objectives. Record your observations.

5. Make more slides using pieces of gill from other mushrooms.

6. Observe these slides using the low-power and high-power objectives. Compare the different mushroom samples. Record your observations.

What Did You See?

The gills had little knobs attached called **basidia**. Attached to the knobs were spores. These spores are easily removed from the basidium and may just be loose on your slide. The spores are small roundish cells. Spores come in a variety of colors. **Mycologists**, or mushroom experts, use the colors of the spores as clues to identify unknown mushrooms. Brown, button, and Portobello are different stages of the same type of mushroom.

All mushrooms have spores, but not all mushrooms have gills. If a wild mushroom has gills, beware! Most of the known poisonous mushrooms have gills, including the very poisonous Amanita (see the warning and photograph of the red mushroom opposite).

Mushroom gills under the dissecting microscope x25.

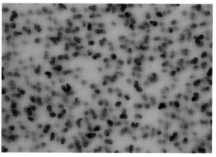

Brown mushroom spores x400.

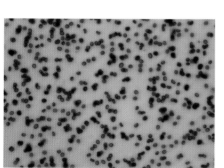

Button mushroom spores x400.

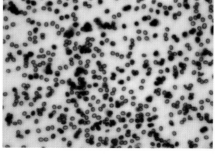

Portobello mushroom spores x400.

Did You Know?

One of the strangest living things is actually two things living together. **Lichens** are both a fungus and an alga. They are not the same as either a fungus or an alga living alone. These two organisms exist in a relationship called mutual **symbiosis**, which means that living together is good for both of them: the photosynthetic algae can supply the fungus with food, and the fungus can trap and provide water to the algae. They can live in the harshest environments, for example, on rocks high up on the sides of mountains.

Lichens are both a fungus and an alga, living together.

They Broke the Mold

When a food has gone moldy, it usually means that it is not good to eat. Molds are fungi and are close relatives of mushrooms. While molds may all look the same to you, there are many different kinds. Blue-green molds are found on certain types of cheese and citrus fruits. Gray mold is usually found on berries. **Rhizopus**, or black bread mold, is usually associated with breads and baked goods, while black mold, or **smut**, is found on vegetables such as onions. Meats sometimes get green mold. And, of course, there's **mildew**, a kind of mold usually associated with gym lockers! So ask your parents not to throw away that green bread. It's a science experiment!

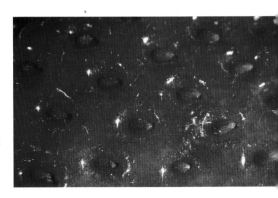

The surface of a strawberry.

You Will Need

Any food mold including those from bread, oranges or lemons, blue cheese, strawberries or other fruit, olives, or anything growing mold in your fridge

Toothpick

Clean slides

Water

Eyedropper

Coverslips

Indelible marker

Soap and water

Warning: If you are allergic to molds, do not perform this experiment.

What to Do

1. Look around your kitchen to see whether you can find any food that has gone moldy. If there isn't any, leave an orange, a piece of bread, a strawberry, and an onion on the counter for about a week. You can also ask your grocer if he or she has any moldy food that you can have as a sample.
2. Use a toothpick to scrape a small bit of mold from the food. Do this carefully so that you do not damage the sample.
3. Place the mold on a slide and make a wet mount, following the directions on page 27. Label the slide so that you know where the sample came from.
4. Place the slide on the stage of the microscope and secure it with the stage clips.
5. Observe your slide using the low-power objective. Record your observations.
6. When you are finished, wash your slides, coverslips, and other equipment with soap and water. Make sure you wash your hands well.

What Did You See?

You saw that the fuzzy material that makes up the mold is really small thread-like filaments. These filaments are called **hyphae**. They are matted together in a mesh called a mycelium, which spreads out over the food sample. The hyphae not only hold the molds in place but also take in nutrients. This explains why molds seem to eat away at the food on which they grow.

You may have seen small dots or thicker sections on the ends of the hyphae. These dots are called **fruiting bodies**, and they contain spores. Using the high-power objective, you may see some very tiny spores. These single-celled particles can be long and thin, or almost spherical. In many ways, spores are similar to seeds. They are released from the fruiting bodies and grow to produce new molds.

Mold on a pear seen under the dissecting microscope x25.

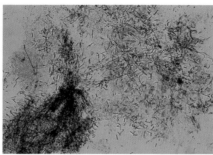

Carrot mold x100.

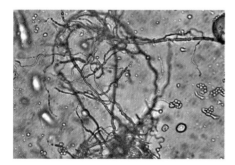

Duck fat mold x400.

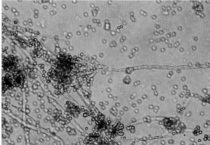

Olive mold x400.

Hot Potato

Many of the foods we eat contain **starch**. Corn has starch, and so do potatoes, peas, rice, sweet potatoes, oats, and other such grains. One of the strange things about starch is that when it is viewed under a microscope, its shape will change depending on where the sample came from. Here is a way of comparing the shapes of different starches under a microscope and seeing the effect of iodine on these samples.

What are these jewel-like grains seen under the light microscope, stained with iodine x200?

You Will Need

Small piece of white potato

Sweet potato or yam, peas, cooked rice, and other starchy vegetables (optional)

Knife (to be handled by an adult only) ▶

Slide

Coverslip

Paper towel

Tincture of iodine

Eyedropper

Water

What to Do

1. Have an adult cut the potato in half. Use the knife to lightly scrape the freshly cut surface of the potato.
2. Place this scraping on the center of a clean slide and make a wet mount of the slide, following the directions on page 27.
3. Place the slide on the stage of the microscope and secure it with the stage clips.
4. Observe your slide using the low-power objective.
5. Remove the slide from the microscope and place it on some paper toweling on a table.
6. Stain the slide with tincture of iodine following the instructions on page 30.
7. View this slide again as in steps 3 and 4. What differences do you notice?
8. Try this experiment using different sources of starch, including sweet potato, rice, peas, and corn. How do the samples of starch differ from the potato sample?

What Did You See?

You saw large, distinct grains of starch in your samples. The iodine reacted with the starch and changed from a brownish red to a bluish black color. The starch grains appear to be bluish black because of the iodine. Potato starch has large grains, which show irregular oval rings that fit inside each other. The other types of starch looked quite different under the microscope. Plants store sugar by making starch. Starch is made up of lots of sugar particles locked together. If you chew starchy foods such as crackers for a long while, they may taste sweet, as your saliva breaks apart the starch, creating sugar.

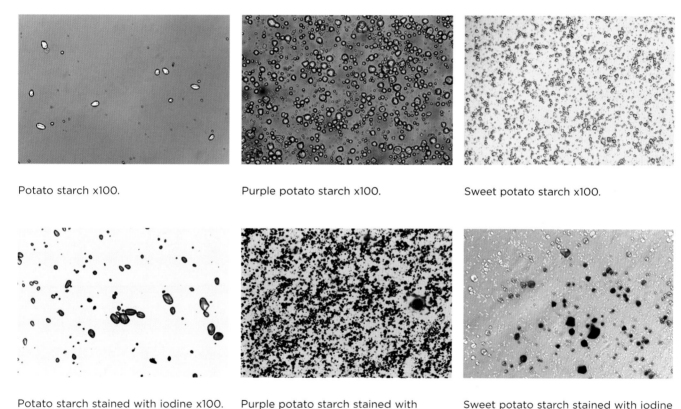

Potato starch x100.

Purple potato starch x100.

Sweet potato starch x100.

Potato starch stained with iodine x100.

Purple potato starch stained with iodine x100.

Sweet potato starch stained with iodine x100.

The Blob

Have you ever watched someone make bread? What starts out as a tiny blob of flour and yeast soon grows into a huge, sweet-smelling bowl of sticky dough. This dough is then punched down, only to rise again. Here is an experiment to examine how yeast grows.

You Will Need

Package of yeast
Large bowl
Warm water
Sugar or corn syrup
Spoon
Eyedropper
Slides
Coverslips
Cloth
Tincture of iodine
Soap and water

What to Do

1. Place a pinch of yeast in a large bowl. Add 1 cup (250 ml) of lukewarm water to the bowl. Do not use hot water, as this will kill the yeast.
2. Add 1 teaspoon (5 ml) of sugar or corn syrup to the warm water and use a spoon to mix the solution.
3. Use an eyedropper to place a small drop of this liquid on a clean slide.
4. Gently lower the coverslip over the drop of water and sample, trying not to trap any air bubbles.
5. Place the slide on the stage of the microscope and secure it with the stage clips.
6. Observe your slide using the low-power objective. Record what you see.
7. Cover the bowl with a cloth and place it in a warm spot overnight
8. The next day, mix the tincture of iodine with some water (two thirds iodine, one third water), so that it is not full strength.
9. Use the eyedropper to place a drop of the yeast solution on a clean glass slide.
10. Stain the slide with the diluted iodine mixture and cover with the coverslip.
11. View the slide as in steps 5 and 6. Does it look different from the one you viewed yesterday?
12. When you are finished, wash your slides, coverslips, all your materials, and your hands with soap and water.

What Did You See?

Yeast, another fungus, is made up of small egg-shaped single cells. The yeast used the sugar or corn syrup as food and grew. When a yeast cell gets too large, it becomes longer and forms a bud. When the bud is large enough, it separates to form a new yeast cell.

The iodine made the yeast cells easier to see. Each cell's nucleus was stained darker by the iodine, and starch grains in the yeast became bluish black. When you buy bread yeast at the grocery store, it doesn't seem to be alive. The beige-colored grains can keep in a tin or foil envelope for many months. When you add water and sugar, the yeast comes alive.

Yeast granules under the dissecting microscope x12.

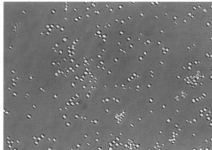
Yeast after one minute in the corn syrup and water solution x200.

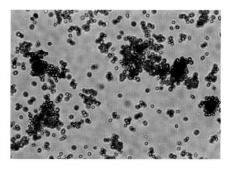
Yeast after 24 hours, stained with iodine x200.

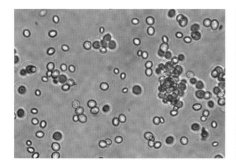
Yeast after sugar is added x400.

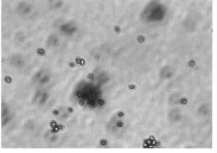
Yeast after one minute, stained with iodine x400.

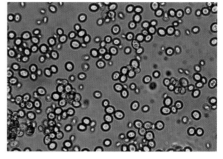
Yeast after 24 hours x400.

Did You Know?

Yeast makes bread rise because as it grows it gives off a gas called carbon dioxide. This gas makes bubbles in the dough. When the bread is baked, the bubbles stay in the dough and make the bread light and airy. Yeast also gives the bread its characteristic flavor. Many years ago, when commercial yeasts were not available, bakers used sourdough, a mixture of flour, sugar, yeast, and bacteria, to keep their yeast alive so they could use it for their daily bread.

Identifiable Culture

Many yogurts that you can buy in grocery stores contain an **active culture**. This means that the yogurt contains live bacteria. Unlike harmful bacteria, which cause disease, this bacteria simply changes milk into yogurt. This is one experiment where you can eat the leftovers.

Warning: Make sure to wash your hands and wipe all equipment, counters, and utensils after use. Eat only the yogurt in the container and not the sample you use on the slide.

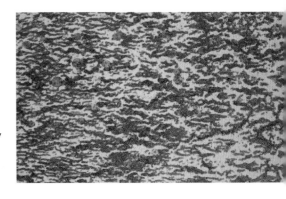

Is there something living in here? Yogurt x50.

You Will Need

Toothpick
Container of plain yogurt with a live culture
Slide
Eyedropper
Water
Coverslip

What to Do

1. Use a toothpick to take a small sample of yogurt from the container. Smear the sample on a slide.
2. Place a small drop of water on the sample to thin out the yogurt.
3. Place the coverslip over the sample, trying not to trap any bubbles.
4. Place the slide on the stage of the microscope and secure it with the stage clips.
5. Observe the slide using the low- and high-power objectives.

Science Fair

Compare different kinds of yogurt and their bacteria. Do some brands have more bacteria than others? Do the different brands of yogurt have the same kind of bacteria? Compare the yogurt bacteria to the bacteria used to make buttermilk. Try storing the yogurt at room temperature for several days. Does the number of bacteria in the sample increase?

What Did You See?

There are tiny rod-shaped bacteria in the sample. You can see them in between the large clumps of yogurt. They are living creatures. There are two cultures of bacteria in yogurt: *Lactobacillus bulgaricus* and *Streptococcus thermophilus*. When they are placed in fresh milk and kept warm, they turn the milk into yogurt.

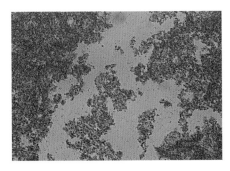

Yogurt x200.

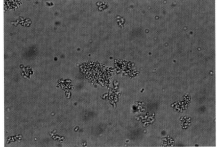

Yogurt x630.

Chipping Away

Researchers estimate that the average American eats about 10 pounds (4.5 kg) of potato chips each year. But have you ever stopped munching on this treat long enough to examine what exactly you are eating? Although this activity may seem like a perfect opportunity to purchase several bags of chips, you won't need large amounts. Ask around the lunchroom at your school. You will need only a small crumb for each.

What is a potato chip?

You Will Need

Different kinds of potato chips
Slide
Tweezers

What to Do

1. Gather a crumb of each kind of potato chip and place your sample in a sealed plastic bag. Label the bag (e.g., Regular salted, BBQ, Salt and Vinegar, Lime and Pepper, etc.).
2. Place a small crumb of each sample on a slide.
3. Place each slide on the stage of the microscope and secure it with the stage clips.
4. View each slide under the microscope at different magnifications.

What Did You See?

Potatoes are **tubers**, which are the underground stems of plants. These tubers are filled with stored food in the form of starch and sugar. While a potato looks pretty solid, it contains millions of tiny cells. Plant cells differ from animal cells, which we are made from, because (among other things) they have cell walls made from **cellulose**.

When the potatoes are thinly sliced and deep fried, the sugars, starches, and cellulose turn a brown color, puff up, and become rigid. This is what makes the chips crunchy. The small bumps you can see in the picture are the remains of the cell walls. Large air pockets like the one near the center of the picture are made when the hot oil causes air in smaller spaces inside the potato slice to expand, kind of like blowing up a balloon.

Regular potato chip under the dissecting microscope x6.

Salt and vinegar potato chip x12.

Did You Know?

Potato chips were created in 1853 at a resort in Saratoga Springs, New York. A diner sent back his potatoes because they were too thick. This offended the chef, George Crum. In response, he sliced the spuds paper thin, then fried them in hot oil and salted them before serving the dish. His new Saratoga Chips were a hit.

Here are some up-close and personal pictures of potato chips taken with a scanning electron microscope (SEM). Note the scale bars: mm (millimeter) for "low power" and μm (micrometers) for "high power" (see also page 87). Even at these magnifications, you can't see the oil on the surface of the chip. The coating of oil left behind in the frying process is too thin to see even with a powerful SEM. You could see bits of spices or flavoring covering the surface of the chip. Seasonings aren't sprinkled on chips, like you would do with salt on popcorn. Instead, the flavorings are applied in a round horizontal tumbler, where the chips are rolled. Eight percent of the final weight of a chip is from the seasonings.

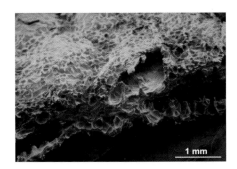

Scanning electron microscope image of a regular potato chip at low power; note the scale bar. Courtesy Dr. Elaine Humphrey.

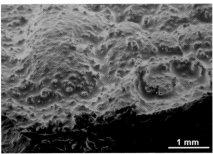

Scanning electron microscope image of a jalepeño potato chip at low power; note the scale bar. Courtesy Dr. Elaine Humphrey.

Why Are SEM Images Black and White

Scanning electron microscopes produce images made by electrons hitting a detector. The electron either hits or doesn't hit, so the images don't have different colors, only black and white. Light microscopes use light that can be lots of different colors.

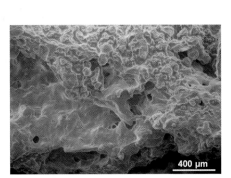

Scanning electron microscope image of a regular potato chip at high power; note the scale bar. Courtesy Dr. Elaine Humphrey.

Scanning electron microscope image of a low-fat potato chip at high power; note the scale bar. Courtesy Dr. Elaine Humphrey.

It's Not Easy Being Green

Plants are probably the easiest materials to view under the microscope. No matter where you live, no matter what time of year, there's always some kind of greenery you can examine. You can look at the grass under your feet, the pollen on the flowers and leaves, or petals to provide all you'll need for studying the microscopic world of plants.

Put a Cork in It

You probably didn't know that the cork from a wine bottle makes a great plant sample for viewing under a microscope. Cork is made from the bark of a special kind of evergreen oak tree. Sheets of cork are carefully peeled off the tree, seasoned (prepared for use), and then boiled before being cut into stoppers. Using your microscope, you can study the pockets of air, called **lenticels**, that the cork contains and see which way the lenticels are pointing.

You Will Need

Sharp knife or single-edged razor blade (to be handled by an adult only) ▶
Round natural cork from a wine bottle
Eyedropper
Water
Slide
Tweezers
Coverslip
Tissue paper or paper towel
Adult helper

What to Do

1. Have an adult cut several thin slices of cork, using the knife or razor blade. The thinner the slice, the easier it will be to see the cork under the microscope.
2. Follow the steps on page 27 for making a wet mount of the cork.
3. Place the slide on the stage of the microscope and secure it with the stage clips.
4. Observe your slide using the low-power objective.

What Did You See?

In the magnified cork you saw air pockets surrounded by thin walls. These are the cells. In cork, the cells look like small rectangular boxes. The cells are empty because all the living matter has died, leaving behind the air pockets. These pockets, or lenticels, are formed in only one direction. The trapped air in these spaces causes cork to float. Corks are cut at an angle so that air cannot get into the wine and cause it to spoil.

In addition to its use as a stopper for bottles, cork is used for many other things, including life preservers, insoles, and even floor tiles.

Cork x50.

Cork x200.

Taking Stalk

Do you enjoy using a straw to slurp up a cold drink? Plants have a way of drinking up liquids, too. Here are two ways of examining how liquids move through plants.

You Will Need

Glass jar or container

Water

Red or blue food coloring, or red or blue ink

Stalk of celery

Sharp knife (to be handled by an adult only) ▶

Adult helper

Paper towels

Tweezers

Slides

Eyedropper

Coverslips

What to Do

1. Fill a glass halfway with water and add 8 to 10 drops of food coloring to the water.
2. Have an adult trim the root end from the stalk of celery.
3. Immediately place the cut end of the celery into the water and let it stand overnight.
4. The next day, remove the stalk from the water and dry it with a paper towel.
5. Have an adult remove about 2 inches (5 cm) of celery from the bottom of the stalk and then cut a few very thin slices across the stalk.
6. Make wet mounts of the celery slices, following the instructions on page 27.

7.   Place the slide on the stage of the microscope and secure it with the stage clips.

8.   Examine your slide under both the low-power and high-power objectives.

9.   Have an adult make a ½-inch (1.25-cm) slice of celery lengthwise from the remaining stalk. Make a wet mount of the piece of celery string.

10. Place the slide on the stage of the microscope and secure it with the stage clips.

11. Examine your slide under the low-power objective.

What Did You See?

The **stalk** of the celery changed color. The stalk was striped because the dye colored the strings of the celery. The celery samples have colored dots along their outside edges. These dots are the xylem cells of the celery stem. The xylem cells transport water and nutrients in plants. The dye in the water shows you where the water went inside the stalk. In the strip of the celery string, the xylem cells look like long rectangular boxes, which make up a tube, very much like a drinking straw. In plants, the water comes into the stalk from the roots, which absorb the water from the soil.

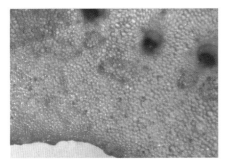

Cross-section of the celery stalk with food coloring under the dissecting microscope x12.

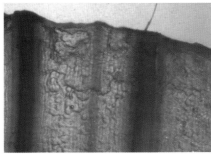

Celery slice with food coloring, cut lengthwise under the dissecting microscope x12.

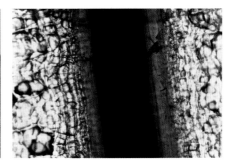

Celery lengthwise x50.

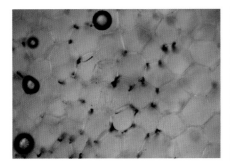

Celery without food coloring x100, with bubbles.

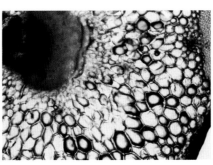

Celery cross-section x50.

Raking Leaves

Plants and their leaves may look very similar to you. They are green and, well, leafy. In fact, there are many different types of leaves. Leaves from different plants are not the same on the outside or on the inside, but they all have one function in common. They are the main location of **photosynthesis** in the plant. Photosynthesis is a process in which plants take water from the roots and carbon dioxide gas from the air and make sugar and oxygen. They use the energy from the sunlight that falls on the leaves to make this happen. This process is very important because animals need the sugar to live and the oxygen to breathe. So take a deep breath and thank a plant!

Fig leaf.

You Will Need

Scissors
**Different kinds of leaves from
    various plants**
Tweezer
Slide
Eyedropper
Water
Coverslip

What to Do

1. Cut a ½-inch (1.25-cm) square from the leaf.
2. Make a wet mount of the leaf piece, following the directions on page 27 and flattening the sample in a drop of water.
3. Place the slide on the stage of the microscope and secure it with the stage clips.
4. Examine your slide under the microscope, using both the low-power and high-power objectives.
5. Make a wet mount of your other leaves and examine them under the microscope, using both the low-power and high-power objectives. Compare the different types of leaves.

What Did You See?

Most of the leaves you used were probably green. The leaves are green because they contain **chlorophyll**, a chemical used in photosynthesis. Leaves that are different colors have other colored pigments as well as the chlorophyll. Some leaves, such as maple leaves, have veins that form a web across the leaf. Other leaves have veins that run from one end of the leaf to the other.

The veins are bundles of xylem cells (see previous activity, "Talking Stalk") and phloem cells, which transport sugars formed by the leaves back into the rest of the plant. Flowering plants can be divided into two large groups. One group, the **dicots**, has leaves with weblike, or spreading, veins. Dicots have two **cotyledons**, or seed leaves, the first set of leaves growing from the seeds. The prefix "di" means "two." Maples are dicots. The other group, the monocots, has leaves with parallel veins. Monocots have only one cotyledon. The prefix "mono" means "one." Corn, grasses, and bamboo are monocots. Both groups contain many thousands of different plants.

Palm leaf under the dissecting microscope x12.

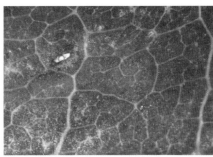

Japanese maple leaf under the dissecting microscope x12.

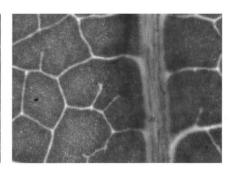

Maple leaf under the dissecting microscope x25.

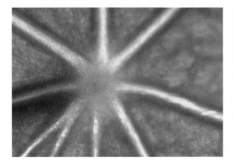

Nasturtium leaf under the dissecting microscope x12.

Leaf from a purple garden plant under the dissecting microscope x12.

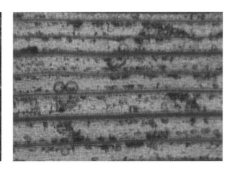

Wheatgrass under the dissecting microscope x25.

Wheatgrass under the light microscope x100.

Did You Know?

If you cut off the tops of most plants they will stop growing from that part. Grasses are unusual because cutting the grass doesn't slow its growth, as you probably know if you've ever seen how much the lawn grows between mowings.

Flower Power

Pollen

There's an old saying that says, "Stop and smell the roses everyday." We feel that not only should you stop and smell the roses, but you should also stop and study all the flowers. For something so beautiful and fragrant, a flower can be extremely complex. This experiment will teach you how to "trick" a flower by **germinating** its pollen.

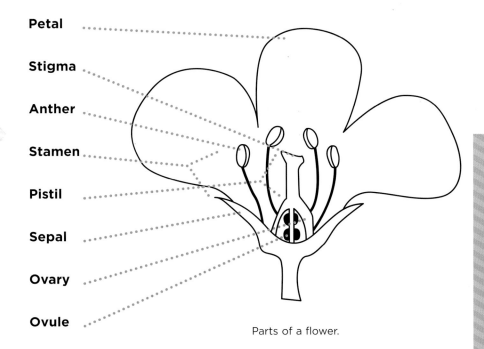

Petal

Stigma

Anther

Stamen

Pistil

Sepal

Ovary

Ovule

Parts of a flower.

Forensics and Pollen

Palynologists, or scientists who study pollen, can help solve crimes. By analyzing pollen grains found on the shoes or clothes of a suspect, they can attempt to match them to pollen or plants found at the scene of a crime. If the pollen is from an unusual plant, it can help to establish a connection between the criminal and the crime scene.

You Will Need

Powdery, yellow pollen from different flowers
Slides
Eyedropper
Water
Coverslips
Pen
Paper

Warning: Do not perform this experiment if you are allergic to pollen.

What to Do

1. Hold the **stamen** of the flower (see drawing) close to the center of the slide and shake the stamen. Some of the pollen should fall off onto the slide. Look for flowers that have lots of yellowy powder on them, as these will give you the best results. If the pollen is really sticky, try blowing lightly on the tip of the stamen to loosen the pollen.
2. Use the eyedropper to place a drop or two of water onto the center of the slide. Make a wet mount following the directions on page 27. Note the type of pollen the slide was made from.
3. Place the slide on the stage of the microscope and secure it with the stage clips.
4. Observe your slide using the low- and high-power objectives.

What Did You See?

Each type of plant has its own unique type of pollen. These pollen grains can be a variety of shapes, including squarish, round, star shaped, or football shaped. Many people are allergic to pollen. In the spring and summer some plants release large amounts of pollen into the air in order to try to make new plants. These tiny pollen grains float through the air, sometimes traveling great distances, even hundreds of miles. If you are allergic, when these grains enter your nose or eyes they make them red and runny.

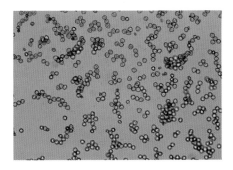

Snapdragon pollen x100.

Easter lily pollen x100.

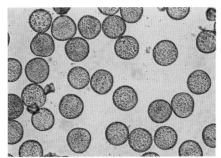

Tulip pollen x200.

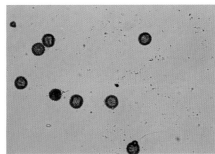

Marigold pollen x200.

Pollen-Nation

Now that you know what pollen looks like, let's change it by helping the pollen to grow a tube.

You Will Need

Sugar
Water
Spoon
Pollen (petunia works best)
Slides
Eyedropper
Coverslips

What to Do

1. Place 1 teaspoon (5 ml) of sugar into 1 cup (250 ml) of lukewarm water. Stir the water to dissolve the sugar.

2. Sprinkle pollen onto the slide as you did in the previous activity ("Flower Power—Pollen"). Use the eyedropper to add a drop of sugar water to the slide and make a wet mount, following the directions on page 27. Record the pollen used and the amount of sugar used.

3. Immediately place the slide under a lamp or in a very warm spot in the house. Watch the slide closely.

4. After about 10 minutes, place the slide on the stage of the microscope and secure it with the stage clips.

5. Observe your slide using the low- and high-power objectives. If nothing has happened (i.e., if the pollen looks the same as it did in the previous activity), put the slide back in a warm spot again. Check on the slide every 10 minutes or so. If you still cannot see any changes after about 90 minutes, try fresh pollen and add more sugar to the sugar-water mixture. Some mixtures of sugar and water work better than others with various pollens.

6. Keep a record of the kind of pollen, the amount of sugar in the mixture, and the amount of time it took to react.

What Did You See?

You tricked the pollen into germinating. When the pollen grains come into contact with the top of the **pistil**, they germinate, or grow. The top of the pistil has a sugary coating; the sugar you added to the pollen acts like this coating. The amount of sugar that will cause the pollen to germinate varies depending on the type of pollen you use. When the pollen grain starts to germinate, it first gets larger; then the pollen grain grows a **pollen tube**. This tube is supposed to work its way down through the pistil to the bottom of the pistil, where the plant's eggs are. The male nuclei of the pollen grain travel down the tube and fertilize the eggs so that new plants can grow.

Science Fair

Here are some questions you might try to answer for a Science Fair project: Are certain kinds of pollen easier to work with than others? How does the mixture of the solution affect the experiment? Does temperature play a part in the creation of pollen tubes? Try a sample at room temperature, another in a warm window, and another from the fridge.

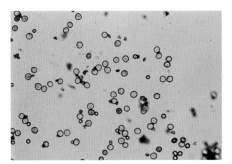

Petunia pollen x100.

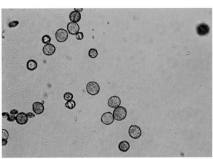

Petunia pollen x200.

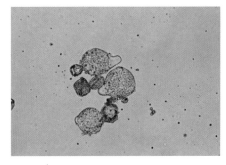

Petunia pollen x400, showing small tubes forming.

Making a Good Impression

Most of the experiments you have performed have involved slicing a sample and then viewing the thin piece of material under the microscope. In some experiments involving thick samples, you viewed only the surface of the sample. Scientists use special microscopes and microscopic techniques to view the surfaces of things such as metal, rocks, and minerals. One way you can magnify the surface of an object is to take an impression of the sample. Here is an easy way to try this at home.

You Will Need

Sharp knife (to be handled by an adult only) ▰

Thick flower leaf or petal

Slide

Clear nail polish

Toothpick

Tweezers

What to Do

1. Have an adult cut a small piece of flower leaf or petal. Place this sample on a slide.
2. Place the slide on the stage of the microscope and secure it with the stage clips.
3. View the sample under the low- and high-power objectives. Make a note of what it looks like.
4. Apply a layer of nail polish to the surface of the leaf or petal and lay a toothpick over the wet nail polish. Allow the polish to dry completely.
5. Peel the toothpick off the leaf. You may have to use the tweezers to pull the hardened nail polish impression off the sample. Don't worry if you can't remove all the polish, you will need only a small section.
6. Place the peeled section on the slide, smooth side down against the slide.
7. Place the slide on the stage of the microscope and secure it with the stage clips.
8. View the sample under the low- and high-power objectives.
9. Coat a small area in the middle of a microscope slide with a thin layer of nail polish. Wait until the polish is sticky but not yet dry. Press a flower leaf or petal onto the surface of the polish and lift off the leaf or petal, leaving an impression in the polish.

10. Allow the slide to dry.

11. Place the slide on the stage of the microscope and secure it with the stage clips.

12. View the sample under the low- and high-power objectives.

What Did You See?

You saw the surface features of the leaf. The cells looked like pieces of a jigsaw puzzle. In some cases, you may have seen the bean-shaped cells called **guard cells**, which have a hole in the middle. This hole, called a **stoma**, allows gases and water to leave the leaf. The nail polish coated the surface of the leaf and seeped into all the cracks in the sample. The hardened polish you removed showed all the details. Some scientists make similar impressions of samples to help them determine information about metals. For example, they can tell the strength of a mixture of metals using this technique. Industrial scientists use this method to view cloth to see the effect that washing and wearing have on a certain fabric.

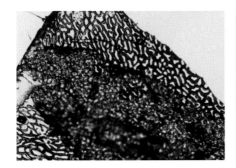

Geranium impression x50.

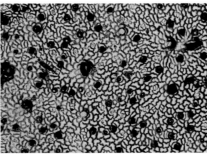

Geranium impression x50.

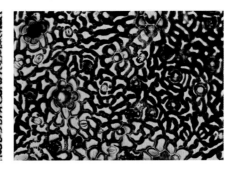

Geranium impression x100.

Leaf Me Alone

Have you ever wondered what a leaf looks like inside? It looks like a miniature roadway linking together tiny towns. Okay, you'd need a vivid imagination to see this, but with this next experiment, you can choose your own words to describe this wondrous sight.

You Will Need

Leaf from a geranium plant
Tweezers
Slide
Eyedropper
Water
Iodine
Coverslip

What to Do

1. Roll the leaf back and forth between your palms to loosen the top fuzzy layer of tissue from the bottom layer of the leaf. As you roll it between your palms, the two layers of leaf will separate.

2. Use the tweezers to separate the top layer from the bottom layer of the leaf. Some people find it easier to peel the top away, while others find it easier to peel the bottom.

3. Cut a tiny piece of the bottom layer of the leaf and place it so the underside of the leaf faces up on the center of a clean slide.

4. Make a wet mount of the slide following the directions on page 27.

5. Place the slide on the stage of the microscope and secure it with the stage clips.

6. Observe your slide using the low- and high-power objectives.

7. Stain the slide using tincture of iodine, following the directions on page 30.

8. Place the slide on the stage of the microscope and secure it with the stage clips.

9. Observe your slide using the low- and high-power objectives.

What Did You See?

The layer of skin on the outside of the leaf is called the **epidermis**, on which are interlocking plant cells that fit together like the pieces of a puzzle. If you look carefully, you will see a pair of bean-shaped guard cells surrounding the stoma. When the plant has enough water, the guard cells swell and open the stoma to allow gases to move in and out of the leaf and to allow water to leave. When the conditions are dry, the guard cells shrink and close the stoma so that no additional water escapes. The stain allows you to see more easily the cell walls, which make up the edges of the plant cells. The guard cells are also darker than the surrounding cells.

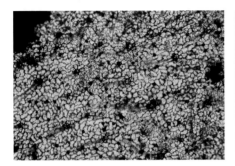

Peeled geranium leaf x50.

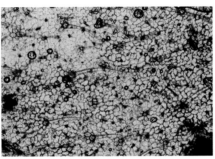

Peeled geranium leaf x50 with iodine stain.

Did You Know?

Geraniums have a very distinctive odor. The scent is stronger if you touch the plant's leaves. The perfume is released when you disturb tiny hairs on the leaves. If you look at the leaves carefully under the microscope, you may see these hairs. The odor may be a natural insect repellent.

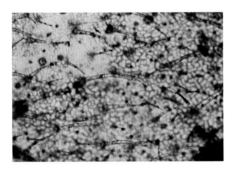

Peeled geranium leaf x50 with iodine stain, focused to show stoma holes.

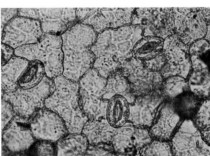

Peeled geranium leaf x400

Four-Leaf Clover

Some adults try to get rid of clover in their lawns. They feel that the clover ruins the grass. Instead of trying to eliminate this plant, adults should try to grow even more of it! Clover is actually good for soil and plants. This plant is a natural fertilizer: The bacteria attached to clover take **nitrogen gas** from the air and turn it into nitrogen compounds, which plants need to grow. To learn more about clover and other bacteria-growing plants, find yourself a patch of clover and read on.

You Will Need

Roots of a white clover plant
Water
Paper towel
Slide
Needle or pin
Eyedropper
Coverslip

What to Do

1. Pull or dig up a clover plant from a garden or lawn. Try to find one with white nodules or bumps on the roots.
2. Rinse the plant off in water to remove any dirt from the roots; then dry it with a paper towel.
3. Pluck off a large, white nodule and place it on the center of a slide.
4. Prick the nodule with the needle or pin. Squash the nodule and rub it around the center of the slide so that liquid from the nodule is spread around the slide.
5. Make a wet mount of the liquid, following the instructions on page 27.
6. Place the slide on the stage of the microscope and secure it with the stage clips.
7. Observe your slide using the low- and high-power objectives.

What Did You See?

You probably saw lots of pieces of the root nodule. You might just have been able to see some very tiny rod-shaped specks using the high-power objective. These are bacteria. These bacteria are called **nitrogen-fixing bacteria** because they take nitrogen gas—a clear, colorless gas that makes up about 78 percent of the air we breathe—from the air and convert it to a form of nitrogen that plants can use for nourishment. The plant can't use the nitrogen directly from the air. The bacteria use the roots of the plant for food and protection and as an anchor to the ground. This relationship between two different types of living things that are found living closely together is called symbiosis (see "Did You Know?" on page 95).

Clover nodule under the dissecting microscope x24.

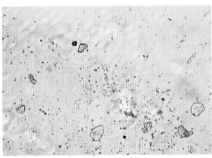

Clover bacteria x200.

Science Fair

Here are some ideas for a Science Fair project: Compare the nitrogen-fixing bacteria to the bacteria found in yogurt or even in your mouth. How does it look different? How does it look the same? Why do you think the bacteria are different?

Not So Dandy Lions

Every gardener knows how difficult it is to grow a weed-free lawn. Despite constant care and tending, weeds seem to spring up everywhere. So where do all these weeds come from? By examining the common **dandelion**, you can begin to understand how and why there are so many of them in lawns all over world.

You Will Need

Several white dandelion heads, milkweeds, or other fluffy-type weed

Envelope or clear plastic sandwich bag

Pen and paper

Tweezers

Eyedropper

Water

Slide

Coverslip

What to Do

1. Gather several white dandelion heads and place them in an envelope or plastic bag to take home. If you are collecting different kinds of weeds, make sure to keep them in different bags. Label the bags so that you know which type of weed is inside.

2. Use a pair of tweezers to pick a single section or strand from the weed. Each single section or strand will look like a miniature parachute.

3. Cover the section with a drop of water; then lower the coverslip over the sample, trying not to trap any air bubbles.

4. Place the slide on the stage of the microscope and secure it with the stage clips.

5. Examine the different parts of the sample using the low- and high-power objectives. Do the "hairs" look the same as the "seed" at the bottom?

6. Examine the seeds of other seedball-type weeds. How do these compare with those of the dandelion?

What Did You See?

After a plant or weed has bloomed and the petals have dropped off, the plant or weed grows a round "ball," called a **seedball**. Inside this ball are the seeds that new plants will grow from when the ball dries out, cracks, and releases the seeds. There are different parts to the dandelion seadball. The hairlike parts are called **pappi**, and they act as natural parachutes. They are light and aerodynamically shaped so that even a small breeze can cause them to break away from the weed and be carried to a spot where they can grow. When the parachute lands, the rough edges of the parachute and seed help the seed stay anchored to the soil. If you hold a fluffy white seedball in your hand, you will see why dandelions are so plentiful. Each ball contains hundreds of potential weeds. The seeds of many other weeds are similar to those of the dandelion.

Dandelion hairlike pappi under the dissecting microscope x6.

Dandelion seed under the dissecting microscope x25

Science Fair

Here are some activities and questions you might develop into a Science Fair project: Using a sealed room and a hair dryer, see how far a seed can travel. Which kinds of weed seeds travel the farthest, and how does their shape affect the distance they travel? Can you make models of the different seed shapes and test them, in a kind of "seed-paper flying contest"?

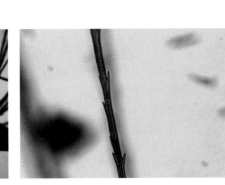

Dandelion pappi under the light microscope x50.

Dandelion pappi x200.

Glow-in-the-Dark Pollen

What do you think a flower looks like to a bumble bee? Let's see.

You Will Need

Passionflower pollen
New paintbrush
Slides
Black light

What to Do

1. Gather pollen from passionflowers. You can find these in many flower shops, especially around Easter. Many stores cut off the pollen and are happy to give you a sample.
2. Use a dry paintbrush to gather pollen and place it on a slide.
3. Place the slide on the stage of the microscope and secure it with the stage clips.
4. Look at the pollen under low- and high-power objectives. You can see that it looks like tiny tennis balls.
5. Turn off the microscope light, turn on a black light near the microscope, and view the pollen again. How does it look?

What Did You See?

The pollen took on a strange glow. As it turns out, some plant pollens **fluoresce**, or glow, when put under a black light. When something shines like this under black light (i.e., ultraviolet or UV), it is called **autofluorescence**. The glow is caused by pigments, or colored chemicals, in the pollen. Plants may use this autofluorescence to attract insects. While you may not be able to see this without the black light, insects such as bees can. Most people can see colors such as red, orange, yellow, green, blue, indigo, and violet, but bees can see ultraviolet. Attracting bees helps plants because the bees transfer pollen from one plant to another.

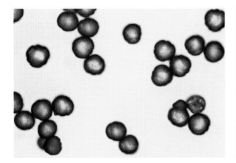

Passionflower pollen x200.

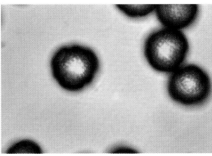

Passionflower pollen x400.

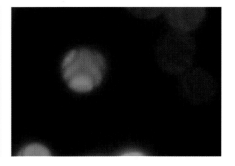

Same passionflower pollen slide shot with UV x400.

Horse Tales

If you had been around 300 million years ago, **horsetails** might have been the most popular plant in your garden. In those days, they were really big, some reaching 100 feet (30 m) or more in height. Nowadays they are small enough that they are weeds that can be pulled out of the ground by even small children. If people only knew how amazing these plants are when viewed under a microscope, they might be less interested in yanking them out of the ground.

A typical marshy, wet area where horsetails can be found growing.

Horsetails with a cluster of horsetail cones.

You Will Need

Part 1
Adult helper

Knife (to be handled by an adult only) ▶

Horsetails, both cone and stem

Paper towel

Microtome

Slide

Eyedropper

Water

Coverslip

Part 2
Adult helper

Knife (to be handled by an adult only) ▶

Cone section of horsetail

Slide

Eyedropper

Water

Coverslip

The distinctive horsetail stem.

What to Do

Part 1
1. Take a walk in the spring with an adult helper and check around marshy, wet areas for a plant that looks like the ones in the photographs shown here.
2. Have an adult use a knife to cut a horsetail stalk. Wrap the stalk in wet paper toweling or place it in a small container of water. If there are any cones growing next to the stalk, cut one and wrap it in wet paper toweling, too. Both these samples are best viewed as soon as possible.
3. Have an adult use the microtome (see page 36) to cut a thin piece across the horsetail stem.
4. Make a wet mount of the horsetail stem piece, following the directions on page 27.
5. Place the slide on the stage of the microscope and secure it with the stage clips.
6. Examine the sample using the low- and high-power objectives.

Part 2
1. Have an adult helper use a knife to scrape the side of the cone part of the horsetail. This should dislodge some star-shaped pieces.
2. Place the star-shaped pieces on a microscope slide and make a squash slide, following the directions on page 31.
3. Place the slide on the stage of the microscope and secure it with the stage clips.
4. Examine the sample using the low- and high-power objectives. When you look at the sample under the high-power objective, see whether you can see the round spores unraveling.

What Did You See?

Horsetails are very unusual plants: There are fewer than 30 species of them worldwide. Despite this small number, they have been found all over the planet. As you can see from the photographs, the horsetail has two separate parts: a tall, green stem and a cone, called the strobilus. The photos show the detail of the cone, with the small, star-shaped sporophylls. The spores are found inside the **sporophylls**.

Detail of the horsetail cone, or strobilus.

When you added water to the horsetail spores, the spores began to spin. They looked like they were dancing before your very eyes. The shimmy they appear to be doing is caused by the unraveling of numerous thin, hairlike structures called **elaters**, which help the spore travel to a new, fertile home.

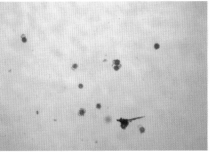

Cone spores under the dissecting microscope.

Star-shaped sporophylls which contain the spores, under the dissecting microscope.

The stem of the horsetail is hollow, with ribs containing xylem and phloem cells around the outside. The stems contain grains of **silica**, a material found in glass and sand. People in some places in the world gather bunches of horsetail stems and use them to scrape or "scour" baked-on food in pots. Thus, horsetails are sometimes called scouring rushes.

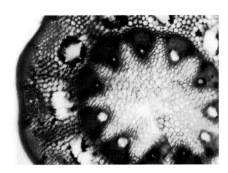

Horsetail stem cross-section x50.

Horsetail stem cross-section x200.

Glossary

Acetone – a colorless flammable liquid used in many brands of nail polish remover

Acids – sour tasting chemicals that react with bases to form salts

Active culture – bacteria used in making yogurt

Algae – a group of simple organisms that have pigments such as chlorophyll but no roots, stem or leaves. Algae include pond scum and seaweeds.

Amphipods – a group of shrimp-like crustaceans

Anthocyanin – the pigment found in purple onions. Anthocyanin acts as an indicator.

Argiope spider – a genus of spiders with particularly large and strikingly colored bodies. Argiope spiders build orb webs that often include stabilimenta.

Arm (of microscope) – the curved part of the microscope that holds the body tube in place over the stage and base

Artifacts – objects accidentally created when a microscope slide is made

Autofluorescence – something that fluoresces naturally or without dyes or markers

Bacilli (singular: bacillus) – rod-shaped bacteria

Bacteria (singular: bacterium) – simple one-celled organisms that do not have a cell nucleus

Barbules – little hooks that hold the tiny strands of the contour feathers to each other

Barnacles – a type of crustacean that attaches itself to rocks, wharves, and boats after a swimming larval stage when it is called a nauplius

Base (of microscope) – the heavy bottom part of the microscope

Bases – bitter tasting chemicals that react with acids to produce salts

Basidia (singular: basidium) – little knobs attached to the gills of mushrooms; basidia contain the spores.

Binocular microscope – a microscope with two eyepieces

Body tube – the tube shaped part of the microscope that holds the nosepiece and objectives on one end and the eyepiece on the other

Calcite – the calcium containing mineral found in limestone, chalk, and marble

Calcium – a metallic chemical element found in seashells, bones, and teeth

Carbon dioxide – a colorless, odorless gas that is given off by animals or plants

Cell walls – the limiting layer of material surrounding plant cells

Cell membrane – the thin covering surrounding the cell

Cell nucleus – the structure in the middle of the cell that contains the cell's genetic material

Cellulose – the chemical that makes up the fibrous parts of plants

Cell – the smallest unit of an organism capable of functioning on its own

Centric diatoms – cylinder shaped diatoms

Chemicals – substances used in their pure forms or in mixtures

Chlorophyll – a green pigment contained in chloroplasts that allows plants to use the sun's energy to produce food

Chloroplasts – small green structures containing chlorophyll in plant cells

Coarse adjustment knob – the large knob on the side of the microscope that quickly adjusts the distance between the sample and the objective (and thus the focus)

Cocci (singular: coccus) – small spherical bacteria clumped together like bunches of grapes

Compound microscope – a microscope that magnifies in two stages by means of an objective lens and an ocular lens

Contour feathers – the large feathers on a bird that give the body its shape

Convex lenses – a lens that is thicker in the middle and thinner on the edges

Copepods – tiny teardrop shaped transparent water dwelling crustaceans that make up the zooplankton

Cork – the outer park of the bark of the cork oak tree that grows in the Mediterranean. Amongst other things cork is used to make stoppers for bottles.

Cortex – (1) the long hollow tube-like part of a hair strand that gives it strength; (2) the layer in a plant root and stem between the epidermis and xylem and phloem.

Cotyledons – seed leaves, the first set of leaves growing from the seeds

Counterfeit – an imitation of a real object such as a bill or document that is intended to fool people into thinking it is the real thing

Crystals – solids whose atoms are arranged in a repeating order

Cuticle – the outer scaly layer of hair

Cyst – a protective covering formed by protozoa that allows them to live in dry conditions for long periods of time

Cytoplasm – the fluid inside a cell surrounding the nucleus

Dandelions – common weeds with yellow flowers and jagged leaves

Daphnia – small water dwelling crustaceans sometimes called water fleas

Denticles – tiny projections on shark skin that make the skin feel as if it were covered with tiny teeth

Depth of field – the distance from the objective through which an object can be moved and still remain in focus

Diaphragm – the part of the microscope that restricts the amount of light shining through the sample

Diatomaceous earth – a clay like material that contains whole diatom shells and parts of the shells

Diatoms – a type of single-celled algae that have cell walls containing silica

Dicots – dicotyledons, the group of flowering plants that has leaves with weblike, or spreading, veins and two cotyledons

Dissecting microscope – a microscope designed to look at three-dimensional objects using light from above and beside the sample

DNA – deoxyribonucleic acid, the compound contained in the nucleus of the cell that carries genetic information and controls the cell's functions

Down feathers – the soft under feathers of a bird

Dyes – substances used to give color to materials such as hair or fabric

Elaters – thin hair-like structures attached to horsetail spores that unravel when the spores are dampened

Electron microscope – a microscope that uses a stream of electrons to form magnified images of samples

Epidermis – the outermost layer of cells on a plant or an animal

Eyepiece (ocular) – the lens system in a microscope that is closest to your eye; it magnifies the image formed by the objective.

Facets – the outer surface of the ommatidia of the compound eye in insects and crustaceans

Fibers – a thread, or structure or object that looks like a thread

Field diameter – the largest distance from one side of the field of view to the other

Field of view – the area of a slide that can be seen through the eyepiece

Filoplumes – hairlike feathers; thin feathers with a single, hairlike shaft. The colorful feathers of peacocks are filoplumes.

Fine adjustment knob – the small knob on the side of the microscope that lets you make small adjustments to the focus

Floaters – small spots you may see when looking into a microscope that are not part of the sample but instead are caused by strands of material inside your eyeball

Fluoresce – to give off light when exposed to ultraviolet light

Focus or focusing – to adjust the position of the lenses to make the image become clear

Follicle – a small sac-like cavity where hair is grown

Fruiting bodies – structures containing spores, found at the ends of hyphae

Fungi (singular: fungus) – plant-like organisms that lack chlorophyll and get their nutrition from other living or dead plants or animals. Fungi include moulds, yeasts, and mushrooms.

Germination – the growing of a seed or spore

Grain (of paper) – the direction that the wood fibers from which paper is made are lined up

Guard cells – pairs of bean-shaped cells surrounding the stoma on the epidermis of plants

Halteres – knoblike structures on flies, where the second pair of wings would be on other insects. The halteres move up and down to act like tiny rudders.

Horsetails – any of a group of plants that reproduces by spores rather than seeds

Hyphae (singular: hypha) – threadlike filaments that make up the mycelium of a fungus

Indicator – a chemical that changes color when mixed with acids or bases

Inks – colored liquids used for printing and writing

International System of Units – the system of measurement that uses the meter as its standard for distance and the kilogram as its standard for mass. It is often known by the acronym SI, from the French name Système International d'Unités.

Lenses – pieces of glass, plastic, diamond or other transparent material that have at least one curved surface and are used to bend light

Lenticels – pores containing pockets of air, found in the stems of woody plants

Lichens – organisms that are both a fungus and an alga living in symbiosis

Light – a form of electromagnetic radiation that can be seen by the eye

Light microscope – the type of microscope that uses light and a series of lenses to magnify objects

Magnification – the amount that the dimensions of an image are or appear to be enlarged compared to the same dimensions in the sample

Medulla – the part of hair inside the shaft that contains grains of pigment, or colored material

Membranes – thin pliable sheets or layers

Metric system – see International System of Units

Mica – a shiny mineral that forms in thin flakes

Microscopists – people who are specialists in using microscopes

Microtome – a piece of equipment that helps you cut very thin slices, or sections, of samples

Mildew – a fungus that attacks plants or that damages paper, leather or fabric when they are left damp

Mites – a group of tiny microscopic creatures related to spiders

Mitochondria – tiny organelles in cells that are used to turn sugar into the chemicals the cell uses for energy

Mold – a fungus that produces a fluffy growth on food or other material

Monocots – monocotyledons, the group of flowering plants that has leaves with parallel veins and only one cotyledon

Mycelium – the mat of hyphae that makes up most of the growing part of a fungus

Mycologists – scientists who study mushrooms

Nauplius – the free swimming juvenile form of barnacles

Nitrogen-fixing bacteria – bacteria found around the roots of plants such as clover. These bacteria take nitrogen gas from the air and turn it into nitrogen compounds, which plants need to grow.

Nitrogen gas – a colorless, tasteless, odorless element that as a gas is the most common component that makes up the air of the atmosphere

Nucleus – see cell nucleus

Nylon – a type of synthetic material that has very uniform fibers that are similar to silk in appearance

Objective (of a microscope) – the part of the microscopes imaging system closest to the sample.

Objective lens – a lens that is part of the microscope's objective

Ocular lens – the lens in the eyepiece

Oil immersion lens – a type of objective lens that is used together with a drop of oil to improve resolution of very small objects

Oligochete – a type of segmented worm such as earthworms

Ommatidia – the dot-like single "eyes" that make up the compound eyes of insects

Orb web – the type of spider web that looks like it is made of spokes moving outward like the spokes of a wheel. The spider uses the sticky fibers of this web to catch small insects, which it eats.

Organelles – structures found inside cells. Mitochondria and chloroplasts are organelles.

Organism – an individual that can carry out the activities of life

Osmosis – the movement of water from areas of low salt or sugar concentration to areas of high concentration

Palynologists – scientists who study pollen

Pappi – the hairlike parts of a dandelion seedball

Particles – very tiny objects or pieces of objects

Pearlescence – a sparkly material used in makeup; pearlescence is made from fish scales.

Pennates – diatoms which are shaped like pens

Permanent mount – a technique that allows a microscope slide to be viewed for a much longer period of time after it has been prepared than for other methods, such as wet mount

Phloem – the food conducting vascular tissues in plants

Photomicrographs – photographs taken using a microscope

Photosynthesis – the process by which green plants create food from carbon dioxide and water using sunlight for energy

Phytoplankton – the layer of living matter that floats near the surface of the ocean and in lakes

Pigment – a substance that gives color to a thing, plant, or animal

Pistil – the female reproductive part of a flower. The pistil includes the stigma, style, and ovary.

Plant cells – the smallest units of plants

Plaque – the stuff that sticks to your teeth and contains bacteria, mucus, and dead cells.

Pollen – tiny spores that contain the male cells released from the anthers of flowering plants

Pollen tube – a long projection that forms as pollen germinates that allows it to fertilize the ovules

Protozoa – the kingdom that consists of about 10,000 different types of single-celled organisms. These creatures live in water all over the world.

Resolution – the ability to see objects that are small and close together as separate objects

Revolving nosepiece – the part of the microscope that holds the objectives, which can be rotated into place

Rhizopus – black bread mold

Sample – the object or part of an object you wish to study or observe

Scanning electron microscope – a type of microscope that uses a beam of electrons to view the outer surface of an object

Seedball – the fluffy seed head formed by dandelions that is made up of dozens of individual seeds

Seed leaves – the first set of leaves growing from seeds

Sensory hairs – small hairs on the surface of insects that detect movement

Shaft – the rigid central part of a contour feather

Silica – a hard glassy mineral found in sand and quartz. Silica is the material used to make glass.

Slide (microscope) – a thin rectangular piece of glass or plastic used as a platform for microscope samples

Smut – black mold found on vegetables such as onions

Specimen – a sample or example of part or all of an organism or object

Spinerettes – (1) a device with tiny holes that is used in the making of synthetic fibers; (2) the small pores that are part of the bodies of spiders and silk worms and that are used to release spider web fibers or silk fibers

Spirilla – corkscrew-shaped bacteria

Spirogyra – a type of filamentous green algae usually found in fresh water

Spores – single-celled seed-like structures found in fungi

Sporophylls – small, star-shaped structures that contain the spores of horsetail plants

Stabilimenta – a heavy zigzag part in the middle of the orb web of the argiope spider

Stage – the flat surface of the microscope on which the slide is secured with stage clips

Stage clips – metal clips used to hold the slide in place on the microscope stage

Stage micrometer – a glass slide with a built in scale for measuring specimens

Stain – a dye or pigment used to color microscope samples

Stalk – the main stem of a plant

Stamen – the pollen-bearing organ of a flower. The stamen is made up of the stalk and the anther.

Starch – a grainy white organic compound that is the main storage for food in plants

Stoma – a hole in the epidermis of the underside of a leaf, which is surrounded by guard cells, that allows water and gases to enter and leave the leaf

Sweat – the clear salty liquid given off from your skin when you are hot or have been exercising. Also the act of producing this liquid.

Strobilus – the cone-shaped structures that make up part of the horsetail plant

Symbiosis – a relationship between organisms living together where both organisms derive a benefit from the relationship

Synthetic – artificially produced, not produced in nature

Système International d'Unités (SI) – see International System of Units

Tubers – the underground stems of plants

Vacuoles – storage sacs for food, waste, or water found in many cells

Vanes – the branches, which grow out from the central shaft of contour feathers

Well slide – a slide with a hollow in the center

Wet mount – a temporary way of preparing a microscope sample in a liquid medium between the slide and cover slip

Xylem – water- and mineral-transporting tubelike plant tissues; they also provide support.

Yeasts – a type of fungus that reproduces asexually by budding

Metric Equivalents

1 meter (m)	=	100 centimeters (cm)	1 centimeter	=	10 millimeters
1 meter	=	1,000 millimeters (mm)	1 centimeter	=	10,000 micrometers
1 meter	=	1,000,000 micrometers (μm)	1 millimeter	=	1,000 micrometers

inches	mm	cm	inches	mm	cm
	[to nearest mm]	[to nearest 0.1 cm]			
1/8	3	0.3	13	330	33.0
1/4	6	0.6	14	356	35.6
3/8	10	1.0	15	381	38.1
1/2	13	1.3	16	406	40.6
5/8	16	1.6	17	432	43.2
3/4	19	1.9	18	457	45.7
7/8	22	2.2	19	483	48.3
1	25	2.5	20	508	50.8
1 1/4	32	3.2	21	533	53.3
1 1/2	38	3.8	22	559	55.9
1 3/4	44	4.4	23	584	58.4
2	51	5.1	24	610	61.0
2 1/2	64	6.4	25	635	63.5
3	76	7.6	26	660	66.0
3 1/2	89	8.9	27	686	68.6
4	102	10.2	28	711	71.1
4 1/2	114	11.4	29	737	73.7
5	127	12.7	30	762	76.2
6	152	15.2	31	787	78.7
7	178	17.8	32	813	81.3
8	203	20.3	33	838	83.8
9	229	22.9	34	864	86.4
10	254	25.4	35	889	88.9
11	279	27.9	36	914	91.4
12	305	30.5			

Conversion Factors

1 mm	=	0.039 inch
1 m	=	3.28 feet
1 m^2	=	10.8 square feet

1 inch	=	25.4 mm
1 foot	=	304.8 mm
1 square foot	=	0.09 m^2

1 teaspoon	=	5 milliliters (ml)
1 tablespoon	=	15 ml
1 cup	=	250 ml
1 pound	=	0.454 kilograms (kg)
1 ounce	=	28.35 grams (g)

Index

Acknowledgments

Thanks to Dianne Gerlach of Carolina Biological Supply Company for her encouragement and kind words. Once again, we would like to express our gratitude to all our friends who saved weird things for us on the off chance we wanted to take pictures of them. You can clean out your fridges now.

Many thanks to Petcetera on Arbutus, Granville Island Flower Shop, 7 Seas Fish Market, the Night Owl Bird Hospital, Maxie the Macaw, James and Liam for their hair, and especially Shira, for cleaning out the fridge to find anything moldy. Murray's Nursery, in Southlands, Vancouver, was especially helpful in locating horsetail samples, and so thanks. Terra Breads on Broadway and Homecraft Importers kindly allowed us to photograph their shops. "Woof" and "meow" to Squishy and Max. And, El'ad, thanks for pitching in with fabulous photography. Our thanks to Dr. M. Schwartzman for teeth images. And thanks to Editor Rodman Pilgrim Neumann—Rodman, you are the best!

Note: No creatures were harmed in the making of this book.

About the Authors

Vancouver author **SHAR LEVINE** is an internationally award-winning, best-selling author of children's science books and science toys/kits. **LESLIE JOHNSTONE** is a freelance writer and head of a high school science department. Levine and Johnstone have written over 50 books and together won the prestigious 2006 Eve Savory Award for Science Communication from the BC Innovation Council. Their book *Backyard Science* (2005) was chosen as one of the best books of the year by Science Books and Films and was short-listed for the Subaru Prize (hands-on activity books) from the American Association for the Advancement of Science. Other recent Sterling books include *Sports Science*; *First Science Experiments: Magnet Power*.